Queen of Sheba: Legend and Reality

Treasures from the British Museum

Introduction and Catalogue Text written by
Dr. St John Simpson
Assistant Keeper, Department of the Ancient Near East
The British Museum
London

Message by
Neil MacGregor
Director, The British Museum
London
and
Foreword by
Dr. Peter C. Keller
President, The Bowers Museum of Cultural Art
Santa Ana, California

Presented by The Bowers Museum of Cultural Art

Exhibition organized by:
The British Museum, London

Presented by:
The Bowers Museum of Cultural Art
Santa Ana, California

©2004 The Bowers Museum of Cultural Art.
All rights reserved.

Printed and bound in Hong Kong by P. Chan & Edward

Design and composition:
ThinkDesign, Buellton, California

Edited by
Vickie C. Byrd,
Executive Vice President,
Bowers Museum of Cultural Art

ISBN: 0-9679612-5-4

Catalogue made possible by
Resources Connection

Inside Front and Back Cover
Detail from CLOTHING APPLIQUÉ

ACKNOWLEDGMENTS

This catalogue was prepared specially for the exhibition at The Bowers Museum of Cultural Art. I am very grateful to Peter Keller, Vickie Byrd and all the staff at the Bowers for their keen interest and patient support of this exhibition project. The corresponding administration for this catalogue within The British Museum was ably handled by Dean Baylis. I am also very grateful to Caroline de Guitaut for kindly allowing us to include one piece from the Royal Collections, and to the three anonymous lenders who very generously permitted the inclusion of their pieces. As always, with such exhibitions which draw on material from different departments at The British Museum, I owe thanks to a large number of individuals. These include John Curtis, Wendy Adams, Jerry Baker, Herma Chang, David Lewis and Jane Newson in the Department of the Ancient Near East; Sheila Canby and Venetia Porter in the Department of Asia; Janet Larkin and Andy Meadows in the Department of Coins & Medals; David Thompson in the Department of Prehistory & Europe; Antony Griffiths and especially Donato Esposito in the Department of Prints & Drawings, who was responsible for writing some of the entries and introductory sections.

Thanks to Michael MacDonald for his written contribution, as well as to A.V. Sedov for use of his entries (slightly adapted), written for a previous exhibition organized with the assistance of the Yemeni General Organization of Antiquities & Museums (GOAM) at The British Museum in 2002. Some of the text for this catalogue partly draws on earlier published works, corrects some statements made in the previous exhibition catalogue, and includes unpublished documentation on provenance and acquisition details based on archival information, and new scientific analyses carried out for this catalogue by Janet Ambers, Caroline Cartwright and Rebecca Stacey in the Department of Conservation, Documentation & Research. I am particularly indebted to Lisa Baylis and Barbara Winter, who were responsible for all of the British Museum photography, with additional thanks to those who assisted them. I am also very grateful to Jude Rayner, Hayley Bullock, Pippa Pearce, Denise Ling, Eric Miller, Michelle Hercules and Annie Brodrick, for completing the conservation work on these objects, with additional thanks to all others who had a hand in completing the conservation work. Finally, my thanks are due to Mohamed Maraqten for his reading of the some of the inscriptions, and Bill Glanzman and Giovanni Mazzini for very kindly agreeing to read the archaeological and philological parts of the catalogue.

Dr. St John Simpson
Assistant Keeper, Department of the Ancient Near East
The British Museum, London

MESSAGE FROM THE BRITISH MUSEUM

The Queen of Sheba has always been a wonderfully intriguing figure famed for her beauty and wealth, although much of her true identity remains unknown. This exhibition of antiquities, coins, prints, drawings and modern ephemera presents a tremendous opportunity for visitors to the Bowers Museum to discover more about this shadowy Queen, and explore the many sides of her multifaceted story through close examination of South Arabian antiquities.

The exhibition has been specially created in partnership with the Bowers Museum, and includes many objects never shown in North America before, and two of the British Museum's newest acquisitions: the brooding etched reconstruction of Solomon's palace by Marius Bauer, and a vivid, inlaid sculptured face of an ancient Southern Arabian lady. Here we can borrow a leaf from the passage in the Book of Kings that has captured the world's imagination by illustrating some of those treasures, the spices, gold and precious stones that the anonymous Queen of Sheba brought to Solomon. Her universal appeal has rendered true the exclamation in Flaubert's Temptation of St Antony (1874) that "she is not a woman but a world!"

Mr. Neil MacGregor
Director, The British Museum, London

Opposite Page.
Detail from OIL ON CANVAS

FOREWORD

In 2001, the Bowers Museum presented one of its most successful exhibitions, *Egyptian Treasures from the British Museum.* The success of this exhibition led to discussions with The British Museum for future exhibitions, and eventually the signing of an historic joint venture agreement between The Bowers Museum and The British Museum.

Queen of Sheba: Legend and Reality - Treasures from the British Museum is the second British Museum exhibition hosted by The Bowers. *Queen of Sheba* is an exhibition that was originally shown in London in 2002 in collaboration with the country of Yemen. This highly successful exhibition immediately caught our interest. Unfortunately, at that time, the artifacts from Yemen had to be returned, and an extension to bring the exhibition to the United States was out of the question. Thanks to the cooperative efforts of John Curtis, Dr. St John Simpson, and Dean Baylis, we found that by drawing on the collections of the British Museum we could recast the exhibition and present the *Queen of Sheba* at the Bowers.

The Queen of Sheba is one of those mythical characters that have stirred the imagination of people for centuries. She is mentioned in Judaic, Christian, and Islamic sacred texts, and thought to have come from Saba, a powerful incense-trading kingdom.

This exhibition explores the modern legend of the Queen of Sheba as portrayed in art and film. It will also explore the legend of the Queen of Sheba and King Solomon as the progenitors of Ethiopian royalty. The second half of the exhibition delves into the reality of the Queen of Sheba by looking into the archaeological evidence from the ancient kingdom of Saba in modern day Yemen. It is very interesting material, without a definite answer as to who she was, as research has only begun to reveal her actual existence.

No exhibition of this importance would succeed without the help of several individuals. Neil MacGregor, director of the British Museum is to be thanked for his faith in the Bowers Museum and for encouraging his staff to work so well with us. The Department of the Ancient Near East, particularly Dr. St John Simpson, assistant keeper, and Dean Baylis, executive officer, who worked for months putting the additional portion of the exhibit together. In addition, no undertaking like this can happen without financial support. I particularly want to thank Resources Connection, and their CEO Donald Murray, for their generous support of this catalogue.

Paul Johnson and his exhibition staff performed their magic, once again, in designing and installing a terrific stage for the *Queen of Sheba.* Nicholas Clapp, author of the book *Sheba*: *Through the Desert in Search of the Legendary Queen*, our curatorial consultant, has added incalculable value to our public program series. Finally, Vickie Byrd is to be thanked for spearheading the process of coordinating the editorial and production efforts for this publication.

Queen of Sheba: Legend and Reality is a rare and wonderful exhibition. We hope to illuminate this legendary figure by presenting both an ancient and modern perspective.

Peter C. Keller, Ph.D.
President, The Bowers Museum of Cultural Art

Opposite Page.
Detail from FUNERARY STELA OF RATHADIL

TABLE OF CONTENTS

Opposite Page.
Detail from PLAQUE DEDICATED TO THE GOD ALMAQAH

INTRODUCTION

"When the queen of Sheba heard about the fame of Solomon, and his relation to the name of the Lord, she came to test him with hard questions. Arriving at Jerusalem with a very great caravan - with camels carrying spices, large quantities of gold, and precious stones - she came to Solomon and talked with him about all that she had on her mind. Solomon answered all her questions; nothing was too hard for the king to explain to her. When the Queen of Sheba saw all of Solomon's wisdom and the palace he had built, the food on his table, the seating of his officials, the attending servants in their robes, his cupbearers, and the burnt offerings he made at the temple of the Lord, she was overwhelmed. She said to the king, 'the report I heard in my country about your achievements and your wisdom is true. But I did not believe these things until I came and saw with my own eyes. Indeed, not even half was told me; in wisdom and wealth you have far exceeded the report I heard. How happy your men must be! How happy your officials who continually stand before you and hear your wisdom! Praise be the Lord your God, who has delighted in you and placed you on the throne of Israel. Because of the Lord's eternal love for Israel, he has made you king, to maintain justice and righteousness.' And she gave the king one hundred and twenty talents of gold, large quantities of spices, and precious stones. Never again were so many spices brought in as those the Queen of Sheba gave to King Solomon. King Solomon gave the Queen of Sheba all she desired, whatsoever she asked, besides what he had given her out of his royal bounty; then she left and returned with all her retinue to her own country" (I Kings 10).

This is the first of two almost identical passages in the Bible, which describe the meeting of an unnamed Queen of Sheba with King Solomon. It is repeated almost verbatim in 2 Chronicles 9, with shorter allusions in the Gospels (Matthew 12:42, Luke 11:31), and in Psalm 72. It implies an exceptional exchange of riches as well as a tantalizing exchange of riddles, and serves to underline the wisdom, might and legitimacy of Solomon as King of Israel.

The brevity of the passage and the anonymity of the queen contribute to the enigma, yet the mere allusion to a Queen of Sheba evokes images of beauty, wisdom, mystery and exotic riches, and continues to inspire audiences from America to Japan. Also known as the Queen of the South; Nicaulis in Josephus' (1st century *ad*) book Jewish Antiquities; Bilqis in the Islamic literature; and Maqeda in Ethiopia, she prompted Shakespeare (1564-1616), to comment that "Saba was never more covetous of wisdom and fair virtue than this pure soul shall be" (Henry VIII, Act V, Scene 5). Her imagined beauty inspired the subject of an Elizabethan love sonnet by George Wither (1588-1667), to be described as "Another Sheba queen." Rudyard Kipling (1865-1936), declared in one of his Just So Stories for Little Children, "The Butterfly that Stamped" (1902), "There was never a Queen like Balkis, from here to the wide world's end." She is even featured in a "Famous Beauties" cigarette card series issued by John Player in 1931. Today, the march from Handel's Oratorio continues to be the most popular theme for church weddings in England.

In Western European art of the Renaissance, the artists chose to emphasize the splendor of Solomon's Court and the fabulous riches brought by the queen. Hints of exoticism were occasionally offered by the depiction of camels, peacocks or monkeys in her train, which were either recognizably redolent of Arabia or other references in the Book of Kings (10:22), to the "gold and silver, ivory, and apes, and peacocks." The figures themselves were invariably cast in European manner, although the eastern origins of the queen's retinue were hinted at by the use of Turkish turbans, and the antiquity of the scene was underlined by Renaissance artists through background architectural allusions to Classical buildings, their only known points of reference.

The story behind the legend is complex and includes a strong whiff of allegory. The subject of a meeting between these icons of wealth and wisdom was not lost on courtly circles; the theatrical setting of some paintings is not surprising, as the scenes themselves were occasionally physically re-enacted. A banquet provided to honor the arrival of Queen Anna's brother, the King of Denmark, to the English court in 1606 turned out to be a very drunken affair according to the account of Sir John Harrington: "Ladies abandoned their sobriety, and are seen to roll about in intoxication. One day a great feast was held, and after dinner the representation of Solomon in his temple...The lady who did play the Queen [of Sheba's] part did carry most precious gifts to both their Majesties, but forgetting the steps arising to the canopy, overset her casket into his Danish Majesty's lap and fell at his feet... [The figure of] Peace entered, but I grieve to tell how [she] most rudely made war with her olive branch... Hope and Faith were both sick and spewing in the lower hall."

Opposite Page.
Detail from SOLOMON AND THE QUEEN OF SHEBA, c. 1470-90

11

Hans Holbein II (1497/98-1543), Court painter to Henry VIII (1491-1547), returned to this topic when he once depicted Henry as an enthroned Solomon at the period that Henry was busy emptying the monasteries of their accumulated wealth. A similar treatment is found in a painting by the Italian artist Lavinia Fontana (1552-1614), of The Visit of the Queen of Sheba to Solomon in which the figures have been identified as members of the Mantuan court, including the Duke of Mantua, Vincenzo I Gonzaga (1562-1612), and his wife Eleonora de Medici (1562-1612). Yet another version painted by Mathias Czwiczek (1601-1654), dated 1649, shows Elizabeth Charlotte von Brandenburg as the Queen of Sheba seated in the center frame, surrounded by ladies in waiting, a brimming treasure chest at her feet, her retinue and camels entering through an arch on one side, and an impatient Solomon seated on the far left. The combination of these attributes together with a Bible story reeked of respectability. Solomon and the queen had thus become role models, and one of the most popular subjects on 15th century Italian painted trousseau chests and 17th century English embroideries. The choice of this scene for marriage cassone was particularly appropriate as the story was conceived "as a traditional bridal procession in which the woman…brings with her a rich dowry" (Marina Warner).

The Queen of Sheba continued to thrive as a subject for Victorian and Edwardian Bible Story anthologies, including one illustrated with a figure uncannily resembling a young Queen Victoria. She inspired two women, Lady Cynthia Graham and Daisy, Princess of Pless (Mary Teresa Cornwallis-West), to dress as her at the famous 1897 Devonshire House Ball (which also featured several Egyptian kings and queens), although Daisy's brother, George Cornwallis, was most unhappy at having to blacken his face and could not understand why "the Queen of Sheba's male attendants were full-blooded negroes and dressed in garments like multicolored bed quilts." The Queen of Sheba now features as an attractive subject for the marketing of glamour and luxury, either through beauty parlors or gourmet cat food, and as an icon for feminists and African-American women.

From the late 19th century onward, this lady begins to become the subject of poetry and light literature. The English poet, Christina Rossetti (1830-1894), returned to this subject among her poems dealing with unrequited love. In 1951, the Newdigate Prize Poem at Oxford was awarded to the Canadian student Michael Hornyansky, for a poem entitled and published as The Queen of Sheba, which includes the evocative words:

"For the wind cries
She is fair, my love; behold, she is fair
Brighter than spiced wine, sweeter than midnight
More secret than the rose. No man may read

Her eyes, decipher the hidden starlight
Fringed in her glance; no mortal mouth declare
Her loveliness. Aloes and myrrh succeed
Her coming, frankincense attends her. Gold
shall adorn her hair, silver shall confine
Her feet, and ivory and silk enfold
Her sleeping…"

However, there is another side to the Queen of Sheba. In the Middle East she was regarded as a much more ambivalent figure. The Judaic tradition, in particular, deviated from the Old Testament account to transform her into the demoness Lilith, and said to be mother of the neo-Babylonian King Nebuchadnezzar, who was hated among the Jews for his destruction of the Temple in Jerusalem. To Josephus, the Jewish historian of the 1st century *ad*, she had the Greek name Nikaulis (from which the Arabic Bilqis was derived), which was one of the nicknames given to the female demon Empusa, and which literally means "donkey-legged woman." According to the Bible "she came to test him with hard questions." Thus, she was a powerful potential challenge to order in a male-dominated society, and the story-tellers dwelt on how Solomon, regarded as the wisest man in Asia, was advised by his own jinns to beware of her powers:

"There's not a man or woman
Born under the skies
Dare match in learning with us two"
(W.B. Yeats: "Solomon to Sheba," The Wild Swans at Coole, 1919)

Successful almost to the end, she was only fooled when, approaching Solomon's throne, she lifted her skirt to prevent it from getting wet on what she believed to be a sheet of water but which was instead a polished floor of marble or glass. The point of this was that Solomon was reassured that her legs were not the full hairy legs of a lilith - deeply feared across the Near East as a child-strangling demon who preyed on women and the newborn - although her ankles were said to be "decidedly hairy." Josephus' reference to her having "donkey legs" or, in later medieval European or Ethiopian folk tradition, otherwise deformed or bird-like feet, all stem from this fear that she was part demoness. This is the origin of the so-called reine p dauque of medieval and later European art and architecture, which include depictions of the Queen of Sheba with the webbed feet of a goose as she crosses a stream separating her from Solomon (a scene later made famous in Piero della Francesca's mural inside the apse of the church of St. Francis in Arezzo, dated between 1452-1459).

Solomon's continuing unease, coupled with her unwillingness to submit to a naked blade, forced her to compromise and use a depilatory cream in the bath (the first to be used in the Near East according to some Early Islamic writers, who described it as being made of a caustic paste of lime and arsenic). This moment of female submission was captured on celluloid by Gina Lollobrigida in her eponymous role in King Vidor's 1959 film Solomon and Sheba, and inspired the marketing men of Hollywood to propose that cinemas mount a bathtub scene in their foyers which "is a stunt which should attract much attention." In any case, although the couple had proved to be finely matched, she acknowledged the power of his god (Yahweh according to the Bible, Allah according to the Koran), and returned to her land. To some scholars, this is an indication that the entire episode was introduced in order to demonstrate the power of God.

But she did not return before Solomon gave her "all she desired and asked for, besides what he had given her out of his royal bounty." Unsurprisingly, this phrase has given rise to some rich re-interpretation. To some artists, Solomon and Sheba were the lovers in the Song of Songs (which is even called the Song of Solomon in the Protestant English Authorized Version). In this, the woman cries, "I am black, but comely" (Nigra sum, sed formosa). However, only rarely is the queen actually shown as black or even dark, although many artists, from Piero della Francesca (1419/21-1492), to John Duncan (1866-1945), deliberately chose to depict at least one of her servants as dark-skinned, and Peter Paul Rubens (1577-1640), and Sir Edward John Poynter (1836-1919), emphasized her exotic origins by adding the occasional parrot or peacock among her gifts.

However, it is the Ethiopian tradition, which dwells in most detail on the union of Solomon and this queen, who is locally and uniquely named as Queen Maqeda (or Magda). According to the circa 14th century Ethiopian history, the Kebra Nagast or Glory of the Kings, this meeting resulted in the birth of a son, Menelik, who was hailed as the first in a new royal line to which the former Ethiopian Emperor Haile Selassie (1892-1975), himself claimed direct descent. Beginning in the 19th century, a colorful local tradition, which continues up to the present day, depicts individual episodes, or a cartoon strip like narrative illustrating events from her life story, and sometimes ends with her burial beneath one of the stelae at the ancient capital of Aksum in northern Ethiopia. As in the Islamic world, there is, therefore, a rich level of local superstition ascribing ruined monuments to the Queen of Sheba and Solomon. In Gustave Flaubert's The Temptation of St. Anthony (1874), Sheba exclaims, "I am not a woman, but a world." How true these words seems to be, as the power of the story of the meeting of Solomon and the Queen of Sheba lies in the flexibility of the evidence to suit totally different audiences. Since she is, after all, reputed to be buried in at least two different countries, as Syrian Arab folklore also places her tomb in the ruins of Palmyra. J.C. Mardrus closed his poem The Queen of Sheba (1924) with the moving words:

> "After a life of splendor and delight, Balkis, princess of marvels and astonishments, was bidden by the Separator to flee away and be a hawk in the sun. So Solomon ordered her undying body to be carried to the pure sands of Palmyra... [The nurse, king, handmaids and finally the mourners lamented the passing away of the queen]. She has departed. The roses have departed. The buds of the roses have passed away. The poppies are gone. In all the garden there is only thorns...And now no man knows where the queen of the South and of the Morning still lives and takes her rest. But her queen's name and her young memory remain abroad to sue for admiration."

Behind these tangled tales, is an equally complex historical picture and series of academic arguments. The earliest reference to a Queen of Sheba is in the Old Testament Book of Kings, whereby she arrived at Jerusalem "with a very great caravan," and presented Solomon with "120 talents [4 tons] of gold, large quantities of spices, and precious stones." This passage purports to date to the 10th or possibly even 9th century, when Solomon is supposed to have reigned, but was certainly not written down until much later, and possibly not until as late as the 6th century *bc*. It is by this period that there was certainly commercial contact between Southern Arabia and the Near East, and there is evidence for the exploitation of gold, aromatics (the so-called "spices"), and precious stones in Southern Arabia. Indeed, the export of aromatics was one of the fundamental components of the South Arabian trade economy, and their consumption throughout the Near East is evident not only through historical sources, but also the popularity of incense burners at archaeological sites. One modern re-interpretation of the Biblical story is influenced by this evidence, and creates an economic model whereby the queen is the head of a trade mission or alternatively, is viewed as a glamorized personification of a wider trade network linking Southern Arabia and the southern Levant in which members of the royal families played a leading role.

There is another ingredient to this scenario, as the exchange of (sometimes unnamed) female members of royal households was a recognized part of high-level diplomacy in the ancient Near East. The anonymity of the queen may allow this reconstruction, but has led to an argument that it indicates a later interpolation into the biblical narrative, as a historical figure would surely have been named. It is therefore difficult to resolve what the intended meaning of this passage is. Furthermore, present-day archaeologists working within Israel continue to argue over the exact date and political (or cultural) importance of the early Israelite King Solomon, and struggle to identify actual remains with his reign. There is a growing suspicion that the story may draw on several strands in order to inflate the importance of Solomon himself. Finally, despite the discovery of many thousands of inscriptions in Southern Arabia, of which many refer to kings of Saba, none refer to a queen of this kingdom, let alone one who traveled to meet Solomon. This is not to totally exclude the possibility of such an inscription being eventually discovered, but the independent archaeological evidence is simply lacking from either region.

Nevertheless, there is certainly rich evidence for the development and flourishing of a major kingdom called Saba in Yemen, which has been popularly anglicized as Sheba. This was the region which "from the great profusion of foodstuffs and other material goods produced therein, it has been named Arabia the Fortunate [Arabia Felix]" (Diodorus Siculus). Through the archaeological evidence, we can begin to glimpse what the truth was behind the poetic reconstructions of "Mareb, the dwelling of Balkis." In the mid-8th century *bc*, a Late Assyrian inscription refers to a raid upon a caravan traveling along the middle-Euphrates corridor, and belonging to: "the people of Tayma and Saba whose abode is far away, whose messenger did not come to my presence, and who did not advance up to my presence: a caravan of theirs approached and who had never traveled to meet me…100 of them I took alive, and 200 of their dromedaries with their loads: purple-wool, 'road'-wool, iron, and alabaster, all of their consignments I took away. A great booty I plundered and I took it inside Suhu."

There has been considerable debate as to whether these "Sabaeans" were indeed from Southern Arabia or whether they refer to a Northern Arabian tribe as the reference to Tayma certainly alludes to a northern Arabian oasis. However, there is no independent evidence for Sabaeans in Northern Arabia. The alabaster appears to refer to one of the most typical products of Southern Arabia, and plausibly, here is intended to refer to alabaster "beehive-jar" containers of unguents, and the "spices" with which they are associated, originate in Southern Arabia.

Saba was the famous of four main kingdoms in Southern Arabia, with its capital at Marib. The other principal Iron Age kingdoms were Main, Qataban and Hadramawt, with respective capitals at Qarnaw, Timna and Shabwa. Each of these kingdoms had their own types of currency, initially derived from a late 5th or early 4th century *bc* Athenian type, spoke their own regional dialects of Sabaean, Minaean, Qatabanian and Hadramitic, and wrote using a distinct South Semitic version of the alphabet. They were also physically situated around the edge of the desert known to Arabic geographers as Sayhad or today as the Ramlat al-Sabatayn. Details of the chronology of the different kingdoms remain to be clarified, but the history is generally divided into three main periods, namely, the Early Sabaean (1st millennium *bc*), Middle Sabaean (1st century *bc*-4th century *ad*), and Late Sabaean or Himyarite (5th-6th centuries *ad*).

The earliest of these periods is divided into two, beginning with a period of rule in Saba, Qataban and Hadramawt (but not Main), by individuals entitled mukarribs (usually identified as "priest-rulers"), until individuals who called themselves malik or "king" replaced them. The first individual to call himself King of Saba was Karibil Watar, and who is dated to the beginning of the 7th century *bc*.

The beginning of the Middle Sabaean period was marked by the diffusion of some Northern Arabian pastoralist tribes into Southern Arabia. Following the unification of Saba, and the highland tribe of Himyar in the 1st century, the Sabaean kings invariably used the title "King of Saba and dhu- [lord of] Raydan" on their inscriptions. Raydan was the citadel of the Himyarite capital at Zafar, and the adoption of the dual title explains a reference in the mid-1st century *ad* Greek source, the Periplus of the Erythraean Sea, which refers to one Charibael being king of two nations, Himyarites and Sabaeans. The latter part of the Middle Sabaean period became politically complicated, as the Sabaeans and Himyarites were occasionally at war with each other, and at times independent kings in Marib and Zafar each claimed the title of "king of Saba and dhu-Raydan." In addition, there were shifting alliances between Saba and Himyar with Qataban, Hadramawt, and the Habashat people on the Red Sea coast.

The Late Sabaean period was characterized by unification of what is now Yemen, by King Shammar Yuharish (c. *ad* 285-300) who took the royal title of "King of Saba, dhu-Raydan, Hadramawt and Yamnat [the South]," while in the first third of the 5th century, the King Abukarib Asad expanded the title to "King of Saba, dhu-Raydan, Hadramawt, Yamnat and their Bedouins in Tawdum and Tihama." This period is also known as the Himyarite period, although the rulers continued to use Sabaean for their monumental inscriptions.

The principal features of the coinage, export trade, architecture, religion, languages, writing, material culture, dress and funerary customs of ancient Southern Arabia are characterized by several very distinctive features, which are discussed below in greater detail. There is evidence for unique multistory monumental architecture, which acts in stark contrast to the Old World norm of sprawling one or two story buildings. The religious architecture was equally distinctive, and a sophisticated understanding was developed of irrigation and field terracing systems, which were aimed at ensuring agricultural stability and maximizing its yields.

The construction of stone city walls around major settlements is a feature of the 7th century *bc* and later kingdoms. These may have been partly intended to exhibit prestige, but the regular campaigns attested in historical inscriptions indicate that fundamentally they had a defensive purpose. These, and other public works, were constructed by free men working under corvée, but slaves are also attested as a minor element in society. The upper classes, royalty and temple administration also owned substantial estates. The origins of these cities remain obscure, but by the 12th century *bc*, there appear to have been an important series of developments. This date marks the beginning of occupation in the oases around the desert fringe in what became the later capitals of the kingdoms of Saba and Hadramawt at Marib and Shabwa.

This therefore implies increasing confidence in the construction and maintenance of the irrigation systems designed to harness the seasonal floods, and which were vital, given the insufficiency of the natural rainfall. The construction of irrigation works implies a degree of cooperation and management of human resources, which may explain the eventual formation of the early kingdoms. It is also during this period that the first inscriptions are found, and which already belongs to a distinct South Semitic alphabet: the existence of these implies the beginning of a written system of recording.

The cultural distinctiveness of the South Arabian kingdoms was partly a product of their relative geographical remoteness. Their distance from the remainder of the non-Arabian kingdoms of the ancient Near East, helps explain the constant allusions to the distances and difficulties faced by travelers. The reference in the Gospels of Luke and Matthew, that the Queen of Sheba "came from the ends of the earth," embodies the position of Saba at the furthest end of the Arabian Peninsula. The economic success of ancient Southern Arabia revolved around its command of luxuries and monopoly of the incense trade, the origins of which were a great mystery even to most of the Classical writers, and it is no wonder that these are an essential element of all the different stories about the Queen of Sheba.

Dr. St John Simpson
Assistant Keeper, Department of the Ancient Near East
The British Museum
London

The Queen of Sheba and the Christian Church

"All they from Sheba shall come: they shall bring forth gold and incense;
and they shall show forth the praises of the Lord"
(Isaiah 60:6).

The Bible contains the fundamental stories of the Christian Church. They could be read either literally or as a series of metaphors of Christian truth, with the Old Testament figures prefiguring those of the New Testament. The illustration of scenes from it within or on the facades of medieval churches and cathedrals across Western Europe was an obvious and powerful means of conveying God's message to their illiterate congregations. The Queen of Sheba's desire to meet Solomon was therefore seen as akin to the marriage of the Church to Christ, with Solomon serving as a prophetic anticipation or messiah of Christ. The chaste queen was also viewed as foreshadowing the Virgin Mary, and her gift of "gold, large quantities of spices, and precious stones" were a portent of the gifts offered the child Christ by the three Magi, who were described as kings from the East. The quote from Isaiah symbolizes the future submission of the Gentiles to Israel.

The official imagery is rich and varied, and these figures often sit alongside other representations of Noah and Abraham. Late 12th century medieval stained glass windows depicting the meeting of Solomon and Sheba exist in the cathedrals at Canterbury and Strasbourg; the scene also survives on the north facade of the Baptistery at Parma, carved by the Italian sculptor Benedetto Antelami (1178-1233). In addition, there are 12th century door jamb figures of the queen on the west facade of the Eglise de Notre Dame at Corbeil and Chartres Cathedral in France, and another added in c. 1175/81 to the famous Norman west front of Rochester cathedral. She recurs at Amiens and Rheims in France. An enameled gold altarpiece was created by Nicholas of Verdun in 1181, and is a rare medieval rendition of the queen as black. Another altar triptych from Flanders depicts the Queen of Sheba on one side, and the Virgin Mary on the other. The apparently random addition of camels or dark-skinned servants as part of her entourage from the late 12th century onward should also be seen as part of the impact of the direct western European exposure to the Near East through the Crusades. Finally, several illustrated French and Flemish manuscripts survive from the 13th century onward, followed by depictions in printed books.

THE QUEEN OF SHEBA'S VISIT TO SOLOMON, 1896
Color engraving

The Biblical story of the Queen of Sheba's visit to the court of king Solomon was a very popular one in Western Europe, but it could also be viewed as an allegory for happy marriage. Furthermore, to a Victorian British audience, it has been argued by Alison Inglis that similarities were noted between the kingdom of Solomon and the British empire, with the "Queen of the South" bringing gifts in a manner redolent of colonial rulers bringing tribute.

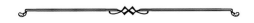

SILVER PAIR-CASED VERGE WATCH, Mid-18th century
Geneva
Purchased in 1958; Ilbert Collection

The iconography of the Queen of Sheba's arrival at the court of Solomon in Jerusalem was popular throughout Western Europe. However, the composition is also frequently confused with another Biblical tale set in Susa (southwest Iran), where Queen Esther requested that the Persian Emperor Xerxes punish Haman for his persecution of the Jews in his name. This watchcase is a good instance of that. It was initially catalogued and published as a depiction of Sheba and Solomon, but there is one crucial difference, as Esther is invariably shown touching one end of the scepter offered her by the king, as described in the Bible: "The king was sitting on his royal throne in the hall, facing the entrance. When he saw Queen Esther standing in the court, he was pleased with her and held out to her the gold scepter that was in his hand. So Esther approached and touched the tip of the scepter. The king asked, 'what is it, Queen Esther? What is your request? Even up to half the kingdom, it will be given to you'" (Esther 5:3). These two Biblical stories share the iconography of a beautiful queen submitting to a powerful king, but only in the case of Esther does the queen touch Solomon's scepter.

The object in question is a silver pair-cased verge watch with a plain silver inner case, numbered 5719, with the maker's mark "EC" incused with a coronet above. There is also a very small maker's mark or import mark "ET" in a rectangular cameo deeply punched into the case back and the pendant. The cast and repoussé (outer case depicting Esther and the Persian king), is signed on the reserve "D. Cochin," although the name is now badly rubbed and indistinct. Inside the outer case is a hand-colored print depicting a young woman wearing a white blouse, a pink dress with blue waistband, and she is holding up a bird in a cage. A piece of red velvet is used as a lining, and the object has a white enamel dial with an arcaded minute circle numbered 5-60 and hours I-XII. It has beetle and poker hands, but the gold hour hand is not original. The gilded fusee movement has circular gilded-brass plates and four square baluster pillars. It has a verge escapement controlled by a brass three-arm balance, and a spiral balance spring with a geared regulator; the silver index engraved 1-4. The balance bridge is pierced and engraved with foliate scrolls.

The movement is signed on the back plate "John Wilter London no. 5719." The name John Wilter on the movement is an interesting one, which is thought to be one of a series of fictitious names used by Geneva watchmakers, either for the supply of illegal second quality goods for retail in London by well-known London watchmakers, or for sale in Europe generally where, at the time, the word London on a watch would add kudos. For many years, these watches were called "Dutch Forgeries," as the arcaded minute dials popular in The Netherlands at the time, were thought to be a clue regarding their origin. However, it is now known that they originated in Switzerland, and specifically in Geneva. Daniel Cochin (fl. 1732-70), began his career as a master engraver in Geneva in 1732, and seems to have specialized in the decoration of watchcases and boxes. A method particularly associated with him is the production of silver decorative cases, using casting methods in imitation of the more common and demanding repoussé technique. Here a master model is prepared and used to make any number of cast copies, in contrast to the hand raised individual pieces produced using the repoussé technique, making it possible to produce a larger number of pieces at lower a cost.

The Queen of Sheba from the European Renaissance to Victorian Realism

The visit of the Queen of Sheba to the court of King Solomon in Jerusalem has long been popular with European artists. The source of this popularity is varied, but the opportunity of depicting an exotic foreign ruler laden with precious gifts (the supposed product of her land), proved attractive to a wealth of painters, sculptors and designers. The episode frequently chosen was the encounter in Solomon's throne room thronging with his courtiers, and the royal visitor with her party discharging her precious cargo. The elaborate drapery and costume of the respective parties would have had a strong artistic attraction. The most exuberant depictions in Western painting come from the Baroque period where the stunning canvases of Giovanni Battista Pittoni (1687-1767) and Jean François de Troy (1679-1752), reveled in theatricality and lavishness. The story of the Queen of Sheba was frequently included in serial decorative schemes based on the Bible. The two most celebrated of these were the bronze doors for the Baptistery of the Florentine Duomo by Lorenzo Ghiberti of c. 1425-52, and the frescoes designed by Raphael for the Vatican Loggia of c. 1518. These schemes were deeply influential and many subsequent treatments of the subject depended heavily upon them.

The Queen of Sheba also had a particular appeal beyond the obvious Biblical narrative or sequence. From as early as the 15th century, the encounter was depicted for its own sake, and an engraving by Francesco Rosselli of c.1470-90 was probably used as the decoration of the interior of jewelry boxes, the contents of which mirrored that brought to Solomon by this queen. Sometimes this regional connection was reinforced by

the inclusion of red coral mined from the neighboring Red Sea in her bounty; thus Jacques Stella (1596-1657) in his painting of c.1650 (Musée des Beaux-Arts de Lyon) includes both raw and fashioned coral. But usually, artists exploited the opportunity for exoticism above all else. This reached its climax in the late 19th century with a work by Edward John Poynter (1836-1919). In this vast painting, some five by three meters in size, Solomon's palace is based upon some effort of historical accuracy and leaning with carefully researched details, such as elements of the architecture, costume and accessories. But owing to the paucity of ancient South Arabian material Poynter adopted models provided by ancient Mesopotamia then especially well known through recent discoveries of 9th century *bc*, and later sculptures in the capitals of the Assyrian empire in what is now northern Iraq. The British Museum would have played a central role in his research, and happily, drawings survive that record his doubtless frequent visits to this Museum. The painting is represented by a number of preparatory drawings and in many ways is the last great flowering of a rich tradition.

However, the story of the Queen of Sheba continues to inspire contemporary artists. Foremost among these is the Brazilian-born London based painter and sculptor Anna Maria Pacheco (b.1943). Her output is varied and encompasses a set of ten hand-colored drypoints for a *libre d'artiste* illustrating poetry by Ruth Fairlight, four of which are based on various aspects of the Christian and non-Christian folklore built around the Queen of Sheba and Solomon; these include the invitation sent by Solomon via a hoopoe bird (*The Hoopoe*), the pool of water allowing Solomon to inspect Sheba's supposedly hairy legs (*Water*), and the familiar moment of their encounter (*Their Meeting*). Four-color monotypes relating to these passages were recently acquired by the Ashmolean Museum in Oxford following an exhibition of her work there in 2001. Pacheco has worked up a number of these compositions into independent works including a pastel *Hairy Legs of the Queen of Sheba III* (2001; private collection, Brazil).

THE QUEEN OF SHEBA, c. 1752-53
Claude Olivier Gallimard (1720-1774) after Jean François de Troy (1679-1752)
Engraving with engraved lettering
Purchased from Colnaghi, London

SOLOMON AND THE QUEEN OF SHEBA, 1642
Wenceslaus Hollar (1607-77) after Hans Holbein II (1497/8-1543)
Etching
Purchased from Mr. Bihn

Hollar's etching, based on a miniature by Holbein, now in the Royal Library at Windsor Castle (cf. The Queen's Gallery 1978, 129-30, cat. 88), was an unusual departure for an artist whose only other work in miniature was portraiture. The execution is exquisite, with silverpoint underdrawing, watercolor washes and gold heightening. The etching after the miniature is equally delicate. Hollar has employed a variety of techniques from cross-hatching and parallel lines to stippling in order to model forms and textures. In addition, the plate has been bitten to different depths allowing subtleties of line and tone. Hollar took great care in his printmaking, and a surviving letter written on the verso of an unfinished proof (in the British Museum) of this print is revealing: "You must not think [that] this is the best impression, because I had it printed as soon as I had shaken off the etching fluid, and the whole thing has still to be corrected…I never let anyone see proofs until the pieces have been perfected." This etching is one of a number after works of art in the collection of Thomas Howard, 2nd Earl of Arundel (1585-1646), in whose service Hollar was employed and the print would have been a fine advertisement of his refined taste.

   The figure of King Solomon clearly resembles King Henry VIII (1491-1547), in whose court Holbein was employed, and the work may have been intended as a gift. It is believed to be the first occasion that Solomon was given a contemporary likeness. In contrast to earlier depictions, particularly that by Ghiberti, Sheba here is given a cold reception by Solomon who makes a mere gesture of welcome. The depiction communicates an image of kingship that cannot be questioned. The quotation (lacking in the miniature) from the Apocryphal Book of the Wisdom of Solomon (6:24) reinforces this iconography: "But the multitude of the wise is the welfare of the world; and a wise king is the upholding of the people."

SIT DOMINVS DEVS TVVS BENEDICTV
CVI COMPLACVIT IN TE, VT PONERET T
SVPER THRONVM SVVM VT ESSES REX
CONSTITVTVS DOMINO DEO TVO

BEATI VIRI TVI, ET
BEATI SERVI TVI
QVI ASSISTVT CORAM TE

ET OMNI TEMPORE AV
DIVNT SAPIENTIAM TV
AM

VICISTI FAMAM

VIRTVTIBVS TVIS

Priuil. Regis   REGINA SABA   H. Holbein inve
                                                      Londini ex Collecti

THE QUEEN OF SHEBA BEFORE KING SOLOMON, c. 1749
Jan Punt (1711-1779) after Peter Paul Rubens (1577-1640)
Engraving with engraved lettering

In 1620, Rubens was commissioned to decorate the Jesuit Church in his native Antwerp. *The Queen of Sheba before Solomon* was one of thirty-nine ceiling paintings, and the unusual foreshortening is explained by the intended location. The paintings were destroyed by fire in 1718 and de Wit's surviving drawings after them (made in 1711-12), are the most reliable record of Rubens' sumptuous decorations. Following the fire, the importance of de Wit's record became apparent, and he produced a number of elaborate copies that served as models for a set of prints by Jan Punt, his pupil. The present engraving is after one of these drawn copies. One set in red chalk is in the British Museum, and two others (both in watercolor), are in the Stedelijk Prentenkabinet Antwerp and the Courtauld Institute of Art, London. The British Museum's sheets are approximately the same size as the engravings. De Wit is known to have made reworked counterproofs of this set perhaps to serve as models for Punt to follow. One of these counterproofs was acquired by the British Museum in 2001, and makes for an interesting comparison. But it is not known for certainty which set Punt used for his prints.

Solomon steps forth from his throne to receive the kneeling Sheba. Her full lips and broad nose signal her African origin. A monkey clings to a small page that amuses himself with a parrot, both animals probably intended as symbols of Africa, while Solomon's impassive guards look on. The string of pearls hung from her earlobes hint at Sheba's wealth and exoticism. For Rubens, however, the principal concern was the depiction of the material splendor of the scene, from the polished armor of Solomon's guards to the voluminous draperies.

THE QUEEN OF SHEBA, 1901
Marius Alexander Jacques Bauer (1867-1932)
Etching
Presented by Jean and Maurice Jacobs, New York

Bauer became well known in his lifetime for his Orientalist work, especially his etchings. He traveled widely, and his extended sojourns abroad especially in the Middle and Far East, colored his work throughout his prodigious output. He enjoyed the patronage of the Dutch dealer E. J. van Wisselingh, who in 1888 paid for him to undertake one of his trips abroad to Constantinople, then the capital of the expansive Turkish Empire. Bauer would produce numerous drawings while away, and these would later serve as the source for his paintings, watercolors and etchings completed in his studio back home. Wisselingh became the artist's principal agent publishing all his etched work and wrote a *catalogue raisonné* of them in 1927.

The present etching was Bauer's second to deal with the Queen of Sheba. The earlier depiction, *The Queen of Sheba at Jerusalem* (1893), shows her riding through Solomon's bustling city thronging with crowds keen to catch a glimpse of the legendary queen. In the later work, Sheba is shown within the royal residence and met with an enthusiastic welcome; Solomon with arms outstretched descends a staircase to greet her, subjects bow in reverence and musicians fill the chamber with dulcet tones. Bauer mainly concentrates on the architecture dwarfing the figures below. He also revels in small details, and has allowed his artistic license full reign, with eclectic sources for many of them. Solomon's female courtiers wear headdresses with searing cobras borrowed from ancient Egypt, pointed arches from Islamic architecture and umbrellas from the Far East. Peacocks, baby elephants and parrots underscore the heady exoticism. Like Rosselli, some four centuries earlier, leopards too have been introduced for much the same reason. This previously unpublished etching was recently acquired by the Museum in the wake of the *Queen of Sheba: Treasures from Ancient Yemen* exhibition in 2002.

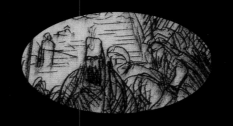

The Queen of Sheba in Popular Western Tradition

"Don't have to humble yourself to me;
I ain't your judge or your king Baby, you know I ain't no Queen of Sheba"
(Bonnie Rait).

The story of Solomon and the Queen of Sheba is one that was ideally suited to popularization. There was sufficient to indicate glamour, riches, exoticism and a touch of romance, but plenty of scope for rich interpretation: film was in many ways the perfect medium as Cecil B. DeMille (1881-1959) once said that a film could be made from any three pages of the Bible, and proved it twice with Samson and Delila (1949), and The Ten Commandments (1956). In 1921, the Queen of Sheba entered Hollywood in the form of Betty Blythe (b. 1893), Hollywood Fox Studio's replacement for the vampish Theda Bara. Sets borrow from those of the epic Intolerance, made by D.W. Griffiths in 1916, as they include Neo-Babylonian glazed tile facades.

In 1954/55, a black-and-white Italian production was entitled The Queen of Sheba, followed in 1959 by Gore Vidal's epic Solomon and Sheba, which starred Tyrone Power and Gina Lollobrigida (b. 1927), in the title roles. Disaster struck with Powers' sudden death on-set, and much of the film had to be reshot with a hastily recast Yul Brynner. "La Lollo" once tellingly referred to Sheba as a courtesan, but the geographical location of Sheba is never mentioned. The opening sequences showing a desert battle between the armies of Israel and Egypt, encapsulated the topical struggles over the then newly created modern state of Israel.

The Queen of Sheba has been the subject of two 19th century operas by Charles Gounod and Kark Goldmark, which were first performed in Paris on February 28, 1862, and in Vienna on March 10, 1875, respectively. In 1932, a full-scale epic ballet by Respighi entitled Belkis, Regina di Saba was performed at La Scala in Milan, with a narrator, chorus, soloists, and an enormous unconventional orchestra, including sitars, and wind-machines; two years later Respighi extracted a purely Orchestral Suite with a combination of a cello solo, furious Arab drumming and a grand climactic "Orgiastic Dance." She has also been featured in Italian cartoons, a recent children's opera written by Marina Warner entitled The Legs of the Queen of Sheba (first performed by the English National Opera in London in 1991), American circus pageants recreated by Barnum & Bailey, and on American television in 1995, where she was played early in the career of Halle Berry, the first

BETTY BLYTHE IN THE TITLE ROLE OF THE QUEEN OF SHEBA, December 1921
Reproduction of the cover of Kinematograph

This was a film directed by J. Gordon Edwards, and intended for the vampish Theda Bara (and star of Edwards' earlier film Cleopatra), but by 1920, Bara's film career was largely over; instead, Fox Studios brought in Betty Blythe, who had begun her acting in theatre as So Long Letty and The Peacock Princess. There was plenty of flesh in the film, but Moving Picture World commented that as "there is never a suggestion of the vamp in one of her poses or gestures," the prudish reviewers would overlook the revealing dress. The plot revolved around Blythe gaining the gratitude of her people for killing her wicked husband king (played by George Siegmann), visiting the court of Solomon (Fritz Leber), where she wins a chariot race, spends her last night with Solomon, and returning pregnant with his son (Pat Moore). He is assumed by her subjects to be the legitimate son of her marriage, but is sent to see his true father Solomon when he is four years of age. There, he attracts the jealousy of his villainous half-brother (a typecast G. Raymond Nye), but the contended succession for Solomon's throne is settled when the Queen of Sheba returns with an army in support of Solomon.

black actress to play her on screen. The fusion of Orientalist literature with the advent of film, Egyptomania and the Art Deco movement triggered a revival in the Queen's fortunes in the 1920s and 1930s. W.B. Yeats (1865-1939) wrote of her "dusky face" and Edmund Dulac illustrated a similarly exotic queen seated high on a camel against a moonlit Arabian Nights background in a series entitled "The Song of Solomon" for the covers of American Weekly. There are also several novels from this period, including one by J.C. Mardrus, a half-Syrian and half-French author and translator of The 1001 Nights, who was the first to compile the different Arabic stories into a short book published in 1924, simply entitled The Queen of Sheba and which begins with the words:

> "This Queen was the flower of all Arabian flowers, a virgin of sixteen whom God had made in beauty. She was perfumed of herself, and by her nature amber. Her waist and color knew no parallel except in Ban branches and Chinese tuberose. Her face was sorcery, as of an idol of Misraim; its cheeks were the shame of roses, the mouth was cut from a single ruby, the chin was marked by a forgotten smile. And there were two long eyes upon it of black and white, sorceries also, diamond and golden; antelope eyes where the black pastured upon the white, in the shadows of the curved swords of the lashes. And each was so long that it was seen in full even when she turned her face aside. When she opened these Egyptian eyes, sighs were about her; and, when she shut them, the world grew dark before the faces of men, and breasts were straitened. This lily child breathed and reigned, white and undesirous, full of pale langour. For she did not know what destiny of love was hers, neither the hour nor face of love. But kept herself aloof, shaded by the bright pearl of her virginity, her mystery of thought. Balkis was her name, a benediction; which the people of Yemen called Balkama. She was Mageda to the Ethiopians."

Only a year previously, the Scottish Symbolist artist John Duncan (1866-1945) painted a vivid scene of her traveling to Solomon's Court, and the Amsterdam student dramatic company performed a play of The Queen of Sheba on November 27, 1923, in the Stadsschouwburg in Amsterdam. Shortly before, an author writing under the pseudonym of "Phinneas A. Crutch" wrote a droll and footnoted Egyptianizing book The Queen of Sheba: Her Life and Times, in which he (or she) imagined the Queen's retinue in some detail: "an assemblage of several hundred personages, satellites and minions escorted by the entire Sheban Guards Brigade… [including] another company of Guards, especially detailed to watch over the ten gilded cages containing the Queen's cats, and preserve order in the twenty tanks of black goldfish from which these felines were fed, an extremely arduous task…" The early poetry tends to emphasize the romance, but the story is later reinterpreted within the feminist genre, and she becomes a thoroughly modern woman who "eats avocados with apostle spoons" when she scours "Scotland for a Solomon" (Kathleen Jamie, 1994).

FILM STILL, LASER COPIES FROM SOLOMON AND SHEBA, 1959
United Artists production with Gina Lollobrigida and Yul Brynner: Queen in chariot;
Solomon and Queen in forest; chariot/battle scene; Yul Brynner as Solomon
with King Vidor, director; close-up of Gina Lollobrigida as the Queen of Sheba;
Solomon and the Queen; Solomon and the Queen in front of the ark
in the ruined Temple; rehearsal scene in chariot

In King Vidor's 1959 Hollywood film Solomon and Sheba, the Queen of Sheba - here played by Gina Lollobrigida - appears as the enemy of Solomon's throne, which is threatened in turn from within by the treacherous machinations of Solomon's brother, Adonijah (George Sanders). Determined to destroy Solomon (and his God) with her feminine wiles, Sheba seduces the king, who begins to fall deeply in love with her. To demonstrate his devotion, Solomon initiates the worship of one of her pagan deities, Ragon, god of love, on Israelite soil which leads, inevitably, to civil strife. Solomon almost loses his throne and the support of his God, who with one well aimed thunderbolt destroys Solomon's magnificent temple (which in true Hollywood style was decorated on the interior with copies of Assyrian palace sculptures, and on the exterior with Achaemenid sculptures from Persepolis in Iran). But realizing that she truly loves him, Sheba prays to Yahweh to relent from his anger and spare Solomon's life and throne. Having done so, she returns to Sheba as a convert to Judaism, carrying Solomon's child in her womb.

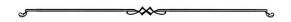

The Queen of Sheba in the Islamic Tradition

"I have just seen things unknown to you. With truthful news I come to you from Sheba, where I found a woman reigning over the people. She is possessed of every virtue and has a splendid throne. I found that she and her subjects worship the sun instead of God. Satan has seduced them and debarred them from the right path"
(Koran 27:22-26).

A different version of the Biblical story of the meeting between the Queen of Sheba and Solomon (Sulayman in Arabic) is given in Chapter 27 of the Koran (known as "The Ant"). The Judaeo-Christian stories must have been deeply rooted in Arabia by this time, as the population of Arabia included significant numbers of Jews and Christians. This was later elaborated on still further by Islamic writers from the 9th century onward, and who name the queen as Bilqis. Solomon was regarded as an early prophet of Islam who was intent on converting the kings of the world. In this respect, he was regarded as a messiah figure similar to the manner in which the Church regarded Solomon as a prefigure of Christ.

In the Muslim tradition, Solomon was credited with powers over all the animals, birds and jinns (genies), understanding of bird speech, command of the winds, and a magnificent builder and metalworker. He traveled

THE QUEEN OF SHEBA (BILQIS) FACING THE HOOPOE, SOLOMON'S MESSENGER, c. 1590-1600

False signature of Bihzad

Iran, Safavid, Qazvin

Tinted drawing on paper

Bequeathed by Sir Bernard Eckstein (1894-1948); formerly in the Claude Anet collection and exhibited at the Persian Art Exhibition in London, 1931 (An Illustrated Souvenir of the Exhibition of Persian Art, London, p. 45, no. 7196)

This drawing depicts an important moment in the Koranic tradition (Sura 27:15-44), when the hoopoe delivers a letter from Solomon to the Queen of Sheba who is named in this literature as Bilqis (although she remains anonymous in the Koran). In the Koran, Solomon is regarded as not only a great and wealthy king with power over birds, animals and jinns, but also a prophet of God. Believing that the queen worshipped the sun instead of God, Solomon wrote to the Queen: "In the Name of God, the Compassionate, the Merciful, do not exalt yourselves above me, but come to me in all submission" (Sura 27:30-31). The queen responded with a letter and gifts and set off to visit Solomon in his crystal palace. In this drawing Bilqis reclines beside a stream, while gazing at the hoopoe that has just landed on the tree stump at the right, holding in its beak a rolled letter from its master, Solomon. Bilqis is shown wearing a remarkable robe which incorporates representations of a hoopoe and other birds and animals, and thus perhaps an allusion to her own potential mastery of these species. The style of the drawing resembles that of artists working at the Safavid court in the 1590s, and has been attributed to Sadiqi Beg, the superintendent of the library of the great Safavid ruler Shah Abbas I (r. 1587-1629). However, despite its narrative theme, the drawing was intended for inclusion in an album rather than being a manuscript illustration.

on a flying carpet, which was shielded from the sun by his vast host of birds. One day he remarked on the absence of the hoopoe from his assembled birds but it returned soon afterwards with the news quoted above. This bird, which appears to be the talking manifestation of the miraculous wind which answers Solomon's commands, then flew back carrying a perfumed, rolled and sealed letter in its beak from Solomon. Her response of a series of rich gifts was rebuffed, so she traveled herself with the purpose of testing Solomon's wisdom with a series of complicated riddles. With the help of his jinns, he was not only able to solve these riddles, but also to borrow and transform the appearance of her throne. She was, therefore, finally forced to recognize the greater power of Solomon and therefore, converted to Islam.

Among the later Arab elaborations on this story are The City of Kitor and the Birth of Bilqis, dated to c. 1100, and attributed to Abu Mohammed ibn Abdallah al-Kisai. In this, Bilqis was said to be the daughter of al-Himyari ("the Himyarite"), a Yemeni vizier, and a jinn, but after her mother's death, she "was succored by the gazelles, raised by the jinns and watched over by the angels. With every passing year, young Bilqis became ever lovelier in face and form. She had the grace of a gazelle and the wits of a desert fox. Her eyes were soft and brown like a deer's but also glinted gold, like the eyes of a leopard of the sands." According to this same account, she met her father and returned to the city, where she murdered the lecherous tyrant king Sharahil; the story then continues along familiar lines until the death of Solomon freed his jinns from captivity, "and this is what has been related of the story of Solomon and Sheba, but God knows best."

SOLOMON ENTHRONED
WITH THE MESSENGER HOOPOE
From Cairo, Egypt 1980s
Polychrome print on paper
Presented by T.J.H. James (b. 1923)

Solomon, seated on a throne surmounted by a large six-pointed star known as "Solomon's Seal" in Arabic tradition, is shown wearing a green cloak embroidered with a six-pointed star, and a crown inscribed in Arabic with the phrase "God is great." The significance of the star is because Solomon was strongly associated with magic, which enabled him to control the natural elements, birds, beasts and jinns. The throne is raised on a stepped base, flanked by pairs of lions as described in the Biblical account, and repeated by some of the Islamic commentators. This elaborate form of throne is also the subject of Islamic depictions in Iran as early as the Timurid period (1387-1468), and continued to be popular through the 19th century. Solomon leans forward to hear the kneeling messenger on the left who points upwards at a hoopoe bird carrying a rolled and sealed letter in its beak. Above the hoopoe are the words that the bird is said to have uttered in the Koran (27:22), and the roundel at the top right shows the congregation worshipping the sun. The remainder of the scene is filled with guardsmen carrying shields again inscribed with the phrase "God is great," councilors in animal-form representing the jinns, and Solomon's host of birds on the right. The Arabic legends at the top state "Our lord Sulayman [Solomon]: On him be peace."

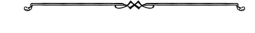

The Queen of Sheba in Ethiopia

"And she arrived in Jerusalem, and brought to the King very many precious gifts which he desired to possess greatly. And he paid her great honor and rejoiced, and he gave her a habitation in the royal palace near him. And he sent her food both for the morning and evening meal"
(Kebra Nagast).

In Ethiopia, the familiar story of the meeting of Solomon and the Queen of Sheba takes on a very different twist. According to the so-called national epic of Ethiopia, the Kebra Nagast or Glory of Kings, the Queen of Sheba once ruled over the northern highlands. This book is generally attributed to a scribe called Yeshaq, and generally believed to have been written in the 14th century or later in order to legitimize the Solomonic dynasty founded by Yekunno Amlak. In it the queen is named as Magda, and it describes how she traveled to meet Solomon after hearing of his wisdom through a merchant called Tamrin.

> "And Solomon loved women passionately, and it came to pass that, when her visits to him multiplied, he longed for her greatly and entreated her to yield herself to him. But she would not surrender herself to him, and she said unto him, 'I came to thee a maiden, a virgin; shall I go back despoiled of my virginity, and suffer disgrace in my kingdom?'"

They agreed on a pact that involved his promise that he would not pursue the matter if she promised not to take anything from him. That night she partook of a special meal prepared with "pungent and aromatic and strong-smelling herbs and spices," but waking in the middle of the night, she drank a large quantity of water in order to quench the "great and fiery heat." This was sufficient for the watchful Solomon to claim a breach of trust, and….She became pregnant but was entrusted with Solomon's seal as a sign of legitimacy, which she could pass on to her child. She returned to her capital, which is said to have been Aksum, and gave birth to a son called Menelik. Menelik returned to Jerusalem to meet his father and is said to have returned with the Ark of the Covenant. His mother then abdicated in his favor, and thenceforth succession was limited to members of the male line. A number of later Ethiopian rulers, culminating in Emperor Haile Selassie (1892-1975), claimed direct descent from Solomon via Menelik and this was enshrined in Article 2 of the revised (1955) constitution of Ethiopia.

(Opposite page, detail; Next page, full image)

Parchment painted with the Ethiopian Sheba legend. Crowned lion on top of scroll with Ethiopian Flag.

Accompanying this written history are numerous highland Ethiopian oral traditions and associations of particular sites, notably the stelae and a large water reservoir at Aksum with the burial place and bath Queen of Sheba, although the antiquity of these stories is unclear. These include reference to the mother of Menelik being a local Tigr‚an girl with the name Eteye Azab, literally "Queen of the South," who was offered together with sweet beer and milk to a dragon who was terrorizing the countryside. She was saved by a group of saints, but was initially driven away from her village until they realized that the dragon was dead, after which she was given the rank of their chieftain. She later traveled to Jerusalem in order that her deformed heel would be healed by him; this it was, but she - as in the written version - fell for a trap as she ate a bowl of his honey. In the popular version, Solomon bedded both her and her maidservant; and Menelik later returned to Jerusalem accompanied by his half-brother. These oral traditions probably embody elements introduced via the Coptic Church of Egypt, notably the use of the title "Queen of the South."

The third set of sources is narrative paintings. These are now the most widely known, but are only recorded from the late 19th and early 20th centuries onward. They appear to be part of an artistic tradition, which began in order to translate oral traditions into a visual narrative suitable for sale to foreigners, exploded in popularity with increased tourism and is now partly exploited locally as commercial branding for Life Insurance and Ethiopian coffee. The earliest known Sheba cycle paintings usually contain between two and eight strips, with a comic strip format becoming formalized in the 1930s. Later versions tend to be less colorful, and include separate white caption boxes; single-scene paintings are also known Sheba's gifts to Solomon, including elephant tusks and a lion, or the preparation of the banquet given by Solomon in her honor. These paintings combine the written and oral accounts in imaginative artistic renderings of the story. The story of the Queen of Sheba and King Solomon is now arguably the most common theme in Ethiopian popular painting.

COFFEE PACKET FROM
ADDIS ABABA
Presented by Her Excellency Frances Guy

This is a classic example of branded marketing of the Sheba story, but in this case applied to Ethiopian coffee sold in the capital of Addis Ababa. The pictures represent the story in typical Ethiopian cartoon strip format with Amharic labels for each scene.

OIL ON CANVAS

This painting belongs to a well-known Ethiopian painting tradition, where the artists sought to depict key moments in the Sheba-Solomon cycle as individual square framed vignettes within a cartoon strip like serial sequence of twenty or more scenes. These were typically distributed in rows or columns. The format probably evolved within a local Ethiopian church-artist tradition of enclosing images within borders, particularly as the first artists to create secular paintings had originally trained as church painters.

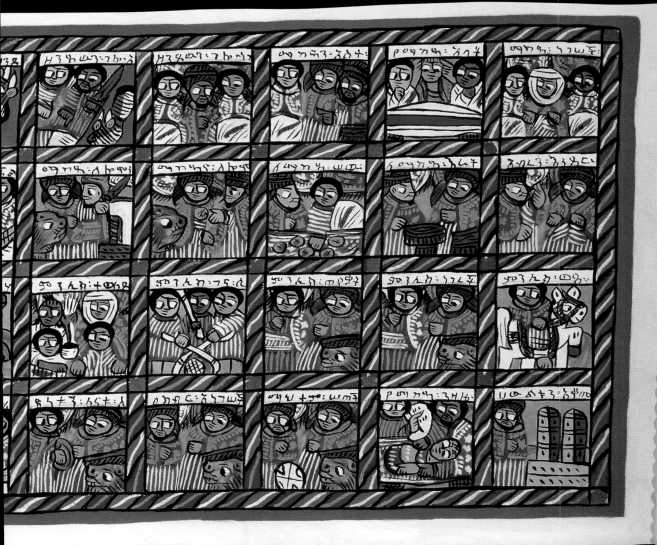

From Antiquarians to Archaeologists: The Exploration of the Ancient Kingdoms of Southern Arabia

In 1767, the explorer Karsten Niebuhr (1733-1815), returned to Denmark as the sole survivor of a five man royal expedition to record the flora of Yemen, and the first person to report the existence there of ancient inscriptions in an unknown script. The Russian scholar Ulrich Jasper Seetzen (1767-1811), copied some of these ancient South Arabian inscriptions at the Himyarite capital at Zafar, but he was murdered shortly afterwards. The credit for the European rediscovery of ancient Southern Arabia is therefore, usually attributed to members of the British survey ship, HMS Palinurus led by Lieutenant James Raymond Wellsted (1805-1842).

The British connection with Southern Arabia begins with the acquisition of Aden by Commander Stafford Bettesworth Haines (1802-1860) in 1838 from Sultan Mahsin of Lahej and Aden. Haines was acting on behalf of the British East India Company, and Aden consequently was considered part of the empire in India. Its strategic importance was significantly enhanced following the opening of the Suez Canal in 1869, as it became an important coaling station on the route to and from India. The British subsequently extended their control over the Hadramawt in what became known as the Aden Protectorate, and then a Crown colony from April 1, 1937 until the British withdrawal in 1967. British military officers, political agents, district officers and other civil servants played a significant role from this period onward in the recording and acquisition of antiquities, particularly from the area of the Wadi Bayhan and the Wadi Markha. Their personal histories and official correspondence offer a useful and still only partly tapped source of information about the circumstances of discovery of many of the objects described here.

The development of ancient South Arabian collections in museums was slow, and apart from a single coin bequeathed by Richard Payne Knight (1751-1824), they only began to be acquired by The British Museum from 1854 onward. As with the development of other areas of the Museum's collections; the Museum Trustees regarded purchase from known individuals to be more effective and less risky compared to conducting

THE EARLIEST COINS IN SOUTHERN ARABIA
Athenian tetradrachms of the "old style" and its "Oriental imitations"
Late 5th-early 4th centuries bc
From Karaman hoard, Asia Minor

The beginning of coin circulation in Arabia Felix can be dated to the late 5th-early 4th centuries *bc*, and was probably closely related to the commercial ties which existed at that period between the Mediterranean world and Southern Arabia. The first coins known to South Arabians were doubtless the Athenian tetradrachms of the so-called "old style" and the local "Oriental imitations," and we may consider these to be the first coins used in South Arabia. According to some scholars, the term balatat/balat which occurred in some South Arabian inscriptions of the last centuries *bc*, and is usually translated as "coin/coins," is simply an adaptation of the Greek pallav "pallavde," referring in the 5th-4th centuries *bc* to the Attic tetradrachms with the head of the goddess Pallas Athena on the obverse.

independent archaeological excavation. The presentation in 1862 of an important collection of inscribed bronze plaques from Amran by Brigadier-General William Marcus Coghlan (1803-1885), then serving as Political Resident and Commandant in Aden, prompted the Museum to rapidly publish a lavish folio catalogue of its so-called Inscriptions in the Himyaritic character now deposited in the British Museum, chiefly discovered in Southern Arabia in 1863. This early collection was dominated by inscriptions and seals. This pattern reflects the 19th century fascination in unknown Semitic scripts, and is also mirrored by the development of the South Arabian collections in the Musée du Louvre, the Kunsthistorisches Museum in Vienna, and the Ottoman Imperial Museum in Istanbul during the 1870s and 1880s.

Aden became the main local market for South Arabian antiquities owing to its concentration of foreign residents and travelers passing to and from India via the Red Sea. This apparently became a source of some contention within the Ottoman capital at Istanbul, where the first of three antiquities laws governing all provinces (including Yemen) had been passed in 1874. Nevertheless, the Ottoman Imperial Museum at Topkapi developed a fine collection of South Arabian inscriptions and other antiquities, which were presented by Ismail Pasha, the Turkish governor of Yemen, in 1880. These were displayed soon afterwards in their former Cypriot hall together with Greek, Roman and Palmyrene sculptures. Istanbul also evidently became an important secondary source for dealers supplying London and Paris. Within Yemen itself, the trade in antiquities appears to have been organized by Jewish dealers in the bazaar at Sanaa who are recorded as collecting, dividing, selling and even faking inscriptions at least as early as 1870. There was an important community of Jewish craftsmen and traders within Yemen at that period, including Marib, and it is therefore not surprising to find that those enterprising Europeans who did travel outside Aden often made use of their services or were themselves Jewish. Furthermore, it explains the circulation of some South Arabian antiquities through Jewish dealers based in Jerusalem. The heavy involvement of this community in the dealing of antiquities mirrors a pattern observed in Iraq and Iran, and partly reflects the close-knit nature of the community, and its established position in the bazaar and commercial procurement network.

Among the staff of Coghlan was the Iraqi born archaeologist Hormuzd Rassam (1826-1910). Rassam had previously excavated in Mesopotamia and Van on behalf of The British Museum, but was posted to Aden in 1854 as a political interpreter. Although there is no evidence that he ever excavated in Southern Arabia, his archaeological inclination, and friendly leanings towards Britain, must have helped influence the high-level acquisition of antiquities in Aden where he served for eight years. Rassam also later played a leading role with Captain (later Lieutenant-Colonel) W.F. Prideaux (1840-1914), Third Assistant Resident at Aden, in the so-called Magdala dispute with Emperor Theodore II of Ethiopia (r. 1855-68). After the departure of Coghlan and Rassam, Prideaux played an important role, corresponding with leading European scholars of Semitic languages and publishing a series of articles in the Transactions of the Society of Biblical Archaeology. These illustrated a number of recent finds and paper squeezes made by French and British soldiers, Christian missionaries, and East India Company doctors, of inscriptions from Marib, the Sanaa region, Abyan and Aden.

However, the means by which these inscriptions reached Aden and Museum collections is best illustrated by a letter dated March 31, 1862, and sent to The British Museum by Coghlan's assistant and Prideaux's immediate predecessor, Sir Robert Lambert Playfair (1828-1899):

"I fear that you have formed an exaggerated estimate of my collection of Himyarite inscriptions - the originals in my possession are few in number and hardly worthy of presentation to the British Museum [though presented they were in the following year], but I think that the collection of rubbings and photographs of Bronzes and inscribed slabs which I have made is unique - unfortunately I am under promise to the owner of some of the most remarkable bronzes, not to give away copies without his authority, but this is the less to be regretted as I am informed that he will himself publish them soon, and make over his invaluable collection to some public institution in England. I have sent in a separate packet by this mail, rubbings of some very fine slabs lately brought from Mareb by one Michael Joseph, a Colporteur [sic] in the employment of the Bible Society, who is, as far as I am aware, the only Christian, with the single exception of M[onsieur] Arnaud, who has ever visited that interesting locality. These inscriptions are still in Aden, and are intended for the Reverend Dr [John] Wilson of Bombay

[1804-1875]. I also enclose photographs of these inscriptions, and of one or two others of my collection, together with my rendering of them into the Arabic character. If any orientalist should succeed in translating them I should be favored with the result. The country round Mareb teems with inscriptions, but it would be a hopeless task for a European to attempt to penetrate that inhospitable region. Michael Joseph, though a native of Baghdad, speaking Arabic as his mother tongue, had the greatest difficulty in doing so, and greater difficulty in bringing away these slabs; I think however that by holding out inducements to some of the inhabitants of Aden, [or] natives of Sanaa, many interesting antiquities could be obtained. If the trustees of the British Museum are anxious to obtain a collection of Himyarite inscriptions, and authorize me to send agents in search of them, I shall be happy to use all my influence to insure success. I would propose that certain natives of the localities where they exist should be tempted by what would be to them high pecuniary rewards, to bring them to Aden, and that they should be paid one or two pounds for each fairly perfect slab. Thus a valuable collection might be made, at very little expense, and even if my anticipations should not be realized, no harm would be done, as I should make their reward contingent on success."

It should be added here that even as late as the 1960s, only a small number of exceptional European individuals traveled outside Aden, let alone as far as the ancient cities of Marib, Qarnaw or Shabwa. One of those exceptional early travelers was Theodore Joseph Arnaud, the French doctor mentioned by Playfair and who was persuaded by the French Consul in the Red Sea port of Jeddah to record newly-reported ancient South Arabian inscriptions. In July 1843, he became the first European to reach Sirwah and Marib, where he described the great dam and ruins of the Awwam temple, and copied or made squeezes of a total of 56 inscriptions. This was a significant addition to knowledge as the South Arabian script had only been deciphered by the great European scholar H.F.W. Gesenius (1786-1842) two years before, and there was eager anticipation for more data.

Arnaud was followed by the Jewish Frenchman Joseph Halvy (1827-1917), who traveled under the auspices of the Academie des Inscriptions et Belles-Lettres in Paris and succeeded in copying a total of 686 inscriptions. He visited sites particularly in the Jawf in the spring of 1870, where he discovered the Minaean capital of Qarnaw (Main) and the ancient sites of Haram (Kharibat Hamdan), Inabba, Kaminahu (Kamna), Nashshan (Kharibat al-Sawda) and Yathil (Baraqish), as well as visiting Marib and discovering another city site at Kharibat Saud en route. Halvy's companion and guide was Hayyim Habshush, a Jew from Sanaa whose profession as a mason must have been of considerable assistance when dealing with stone inscriptions.

The next traveler to undertake serious research was the Austrian scholar Sir Eduard Glaser (1852-1908) who, under the cover of a Muslim doctor of religious science, conducted four expeditions to Yemen between 1882 and 1894. Glaser failed to reach the Jawf, but nevertheless extensively surveyed the Yemeni highlands, and the regions between Sanaa and Marib, and Sanaa and Aden. During the course of these trips he collected or recorded a total of 1,032 inscriptions. He subsequently sold his collection to The British Museum and other European institutions. During the same period, Mr. and Mrs. Bent traveled through the Hadhramawt in 1893/94 (where they acquired several inscriptions). They had previously taken up a proposal to excavate Bronze Age burial mounds in Bahrain, were regarded with great suspicion by French officials in Iran as being agents of The British Museum, and continued from Aden to travel in East Africa, where they recorded South Arabian inscriptions at the site of Yeha in Ethiopia.

However, the first archaeological excavations to be conducted within Southern Arabia itself were carried out in 1927/28 by Carl Rathjens and Hermann von Wissmann at the site of a temple dedicated to the goddess dhat-Badanum at Huqqa, some 23 km. north of Sanaa. Rathjens carried out three further expeditions to the highlands in 1931, 1934 and 1937/38, noting sites and their architectural details, and acquiring inscriptions. The British attempts to pacify tribes in the Hadramawt, under what became known as "Ingrams' Peace," also opened a brief window of opportunity in that region. Gertrude Caton-Thompson (1888-1985), therefore excavated at the site of Huraydah (ancient Madabum) in the Hadramawt from December 1937 to March 1938. This provided the plan of another temple, initially believed to be dedicated to the Semitic moon-god Sin but was subsequently recognized as a temple of the god Sayyin, plus an important published assemblage of human remains, pottery and other finds in two cave-tombs. During the same year, Major R.A.B. Hamilton, later Lord Belhaven and Stenton, excavated the basement of a tower-house at Shabwa, although he mistook the remains to be those of a funerary complex owing to the lack of connecting doorways, and what he believed to be human bones. Among his finds from this building, which are now in the Ashmolean Museum in Oxford, is a fragmentary gypsum slab depicting a rider with a billowing lionskin and an unusual inked inscription. During the same decade, observations were made on ancient routes and sites throughout the Aden Protectorate by, among others, H. St J. Philby (1885-1960), the travel-writer Freya Stark (1893-1993), her former husband, civil servant and author Stewart Perowne (1901-1989), the Political Officer Harold Ingrams and his wife Doreen, Daniel van der Meulen and Hermann von Wissmann. The invention of aerial photography and the support of British Royal Air Force officers based in Aden were of particular assistance in this mapping.

Following the Second World War, scholars began to resume fieldwork in Southern Arabia. The Egyptian scholar Ahmad Fakhry followed an earlier visit by his compatriot M. Tawfik to Main and the Jawf in 1944/45, with a photographic survey of sites and their inscriptions in northern Yemen. In 1951/52, a survey was made by G. J. Ryckmans, Philby and G. Lippens of equivalent sites across the border in western Saudi Arabia, where they recorded a number of Sabaean inscriptions. In 1950, the American Foundation for the Study of Man, directed by Wendell Phillips, joined the Old Testament scholar Frank P. Albright to finally test the veracity of the Biblical account of the Queen of Sheba through excavations. They were the first team to excavate at Marib, namely the peristyle hall entrance to the Awwam temple and part of the adacent cemetery, but the prominent mound believed to mark the actual site of the Sabaean capital remained untouched beneath a modern village. These excavations came to an abrupt end owing to political differences, but the expedition also excavated at the Qatabanian capital of Timna, the nearby cemetery at Hayd ibn Aqil, and the town-site at Hajar ibn Humayd situated in the Wadi Bayhan some 11.5 km. to the south. The last of these sites provided the first section through a long sequence of consecutive settlement layers spanning the late 2nd millennium to the 4th or 5th century *ad*, and supported by the first application of radiocarbon dating in Southern Arabia. The early date suggested for the beginning of the sequence was initially regarded as very controversial as they contradicted the prevalent "short chronology" hypothesis argued by the French scholar Jacqueline Pirenne (1918-1990), whereby the monumental South Arabian script was believed to be derived from that of early 5th century Greece, and the sculpture was thought to be influenced by Greco-Persian types. One result has been the raising of dates previously assigned to inscriptions and objects, and another has been to demonstrate a longer and more complex pattern of cultural development within this region.

During 1959/60, a preliminary archaeological survey of the Hadramawt was carried out by Gerald Lankester Harding (1901-1979), a small museum was opened in Aden in 1966, and attempts were made to regulate the export of antiquities. However, the unstable political situation, which culminated in the British withdrawal in 1967, prevented any further serious archaeological activity until the 1970s. Local, European and North American archaeologists have since been working in most parts of the country with many significant results. One of the most important discoveries has been the recognition of an indigenous Bronze Age culture dating from the 3rd and 2nd millennia *bc*. This culture was responsible for the construction of walled towns and for the manufacture of simple metal tools and weapons in the central highlands, a region previously regarded as having been one of the least advanced. Likewise, the discovery that the huge sprawling settlement site at Sabr, situated some 25 km. north of Aden, may have been founded as early as the late 3rd millennium *bc* suddenly highlights the greater antiquity of this coastal region and potentially its connections with East Africa on the opposite side of the Gulf of Aden. The discovery also of sorghum in a store-room, which was radiocarbon dated to the 9th century *bc*, adds considerably to the debate over the early history of a crop traditionally believed to originate in Ethiopia. The discovery of this previously unsuspected local Bronze Age now offers a much longer cultural sequence in Southern Arabia.

Arguably the second most important development in recent decades has been the discovery and gradual decipherment since the 1970s of thousands of wooden sticks inscribed in a new South Arabian script, which is already adding considerable new information on technical vocabulary and everyday transactions. The wider application of environmental archaeology, landscape survey and radiocarbon dating is providing more reliable evidence for the variety of crops produced, scale of rural settlement, and absolute chronology of sites.

The archaeological potential of Yemen is therefore huge but still only barely explored. There are still many unresolved problems, particularly over the chronology of sites and the material culture, and some of the dates and conclusions suggested in this catalogue are certain to be revised. However, this is the nature of archaeological research and it is sincerely hoped that in the meantime, this exhibition will have raised awareness of the richness of the ancient kingdoms of Southern Arabia whose lasting legacy to world culture has been the story of the Queen of Sheba.

The Coinage of Ancient Southern Arabia

"Mouza [is] an established mart beside the sea...The whole place is full of Arabs, shipmasters and sailors, and hums with business; for they use their own ships for commerce with the opposite coast [of the Red Sea] and with Barygaza [in India]"
(Periplus).

The existence and development of a distinctive coinage in ancient Southern Arabia from the late 5th or early 4th century *bc* onward, offers a tantalizing hint of the commercial transactions carried out in the ports and cities of this region.

The first pre-Islamic South Arabian coin was published in 1868 by A. de Longprier, yet despite subsequent publications from the late 19th century by several eminent scholars, the numismatic study of this part of the ancient Near East still remains in the phase of data collection. The most important of the early numismatic studies on pre-Islamic South Arabian coinage was without doubt, the British Museum Catalogue of the Greek Coins of Arabia, Mesopotamia and Persia in 1922. In preparing this fundamental volume, G.F. Hill had studied all known South Arabian issues from the major European museums. A new phase of South Arabian numismatic studies began in the 1980s when coins from different regions of Yemen, including several very important hoards, surfaced in private and public collections or through the hands of dealers. At the same time numerous archaeological reports brought to light important finds, including those from Khawr Ruri (ancient Sumhuram), Shabwa (ancient Shabwat, the capital of the kingdom of Hadramawt), Bir Ali settlement (ancient Qana) and sites in the Yemeni highlands. Only recently do we have a corpus which assesses purely numismatic aspects such as typology, iconography and weight standard, together with historical and epigraphic studies.

For a long period, the numismatic material from South Arabia was classified in general terms as South Arabian coinage and very rarely definitions such as "Sabaean coinage," "Himyarite coinage," "Qatabanian" or "Himyarite-Qatabanian series," or "Hadrami coinage" were used. However, the "national" coinage of the different South Arabian kingdoms can now be defined more precisely. The names Harib, Raydan and Shaqar on the reverse of the coins, which designate the respective names of the royal residences in Qataban, Himyar and Hadramawt, can be considered to be the names of the royal mints, denoting at the same time the "nationality" of coinage, and the mintage of different South Arabian states. The so-called "twisted oblong symbol," the symbol of the supreme Sabaean god Almaqah and the so-called "signs of Sabaean mukarribs" may have had a similar function for Sabaean coinage, but the identification of the monograms found on coins is again rather controversial.

The chronology of South Arabian coinage has been the subject of much controversy. However, we at least have a terminus post quem for the early imitation series, although the dating of the pieces with only local iconography is very uncertain. There are no dates or other chronological indicators on the coin legends. Furthermore, there are very few iconographic features that can be compared with the well-established chronology of elements of Hellenistic or Roman coinage. There are no excavated coin hoards from South Arabia which have dated foreign series in addition to the local ones. The names of the rulers, who issued South Arabian coins, where they do occur, are very rare and it is difficult to correlate them with the rulers attested in South Arabian inscriptions. Thus, the only means of arriving at an approximate chronology of South Arabian coinage is with the aid of archaeology, when South Arabian coins have been recovered from independently dated archaeological strata.

THE COINAGE OF QATABAN

Series with two heads
Qataban
2nd century bc

Probably around the early 2nd century *bc*, the "Qatabanian owls" were replaced by the series with local iconography. The obverse bore now a beardless male head with short curly hair and the reverse a bearded male head in "Hellenized" style, with hair taken up behind in a kind of chignon. The image on the reverse was usually accompanied with monograms, letters and symbols. The ruler who made those changes put his name Yadaab, and his title "King of Qataban," or the words "King of Qataban set up" on the obverse and reverse of the earliest coins in the series. He may be identified either with Yadaab Dhubayan Yuhargib or with Yadaab Dhubayan Yuhanim, both attested through inscriptions as being kings of Qataban. It is also believed that the same individual also replaced the royal monogram with the name of Harib, the name of his royal residence and, probably, the royal mint, in the exergue on the reverse of the last issues in the series.

COINAGE OF HIMYAR

The Himyarite kingdom seems to have started minting its coins in the late 2nd century *bc*, copying details of the contemporary Qatabanian series with the male head with curly hair on the obverse and the male head with chignon on the reverse. Only a few differences must be pointed out: the name of Raydan in the exergue on the reverse, which denoted the royal mint, various monograms and symbols, which differ from the Qatabanian series, and the "Arabicised" style of the head with chignon. The year 115 *bc* or, alternatively, 110 *bc* may have marked not only the beginning of the so-called Himyarite era but also a starting point for the new coinage.

Series with two heads
Coinage of different rulers of the 1st-2nd centuries ad
Himyar
Silver

Rather soon, and again as in Qataban, the early Himyarite series were replaced by a "series with two heads." The obverse displayed a beardless male head with the "South Arabian hair-style," probably the king's portrait and sometimes accompanied by a monogram. The reverse showed a similar but smaller head supplemented by the name of Raydan in the exergue, the king's name around the top, and another monogram and/or a kind of symbol of the ruling dynasty on either side. The following kings' names are known from the coin legends: Karibil Yuhanim, Amdan Yuhaqbid, Amdan Bayan, Shammar Yuhanim, and Tharan Yaub. The coins of smaller denominations sometimes showed a monogram instead of a head on the obverse, and a shortened king's or mint name, Yaub, Watar or Naam, in the exergue on the reverse. Himyarite pieces, unlike the Qatabanian ones, were usually very scyphate.

Almost all names occurring in the coin legends can be related to Himyarite rulers of the 1st and 2nd centuries, *ad* and who are attested in South Arabian inscriptions. It is quite certain, for instance, that coins with the names of Amdan Yuhaqbid and Amdan Bayan were struck by one person, namely Amdan Bayan Yuhaqbid, King of Saba and dhu-Raydan (c. *ad* 60-70 or 80-100). On the other hand, these coins are very numerous, and this fact may indeed indicate that they continued to circulate widely as a "fossilized coinage" during the reigns of several later Himyarite rulers of the 2nd century *ad*. Coins with the name of Tharan Yaub are associated with Tharan Yaub, King of Saba and dhu-Raydan, who probably reigned in the late 2nd century or more likely the early 3rd century *ad*. It appears that these pieces were the latest in the Himyarite "pre-Imperial" coinage bearing the king's name.

Front   Back

Front

Back

Incense & Trade

"The chief products of Arabia are frankincense and myrrh"
(Pliny).

Smell is one of our five key senses, and a market for perfumes and incense is known to have existed in the ancient Near East and Egypt since at least the 3rd millennium *bc*. However, it is in the 1st millennium *bc* that historical sources begin to refer to an Arabian origin for these, and which are sometimes referred to under the catchall phrase of "spices." During the 8th century *bc*, the Mesopotamian ruler Tiglath-pileser III (744-727 BC) seized "5000 bags of all kinds of spices" from one Shamsi "queen of the Arabs" and received "all kinds of spices" as tribute from "the people of Massa, Tayma [in northern Arabia] and Saba [Biblical Sheba]." From the 7th century *bc* onward, Israelite and Greek sources begin to refer to frankincense and myrrh, both of which originate in Southern Arabia, although their mysterious origins continued to intrigue and baffle later Classical writers. During the 5th century *bc*, the Greek historian Herodotus described the annual consumption of 25 tons of Arabian frankincense as a "voluntary tribute" to Persia, and the 1st century *ad* Roman writer Pliny commented on how the quantity of frankincense burned by the Emperor Nero during the funeral rites for his consort Poppaea exceeded an entire year's production: "Then reckon up the vast number of funerals celebrated yearly throughout the entire world, and the perfumes such as are given to the gods a grain at a time, that are piled up in heaps to the honor of dead bodies!" It is no surprise to therefore find a growing demand for sweet-smelling substances in periods of strong economic development within an overwhelming environment of hot summers, scanty availability of piped water and, during the Roman period, the cremation of the dead.

Perfume and incense were specialities of ancient Southern Arabia, and formed a fundamental part of its trade economy. Herodotus was the first foreign writer to evoke the senses of his audience by writing that: "Arabia...is the one country on earth for growing myrrh and cassia and cinnamon and gum labdanum...

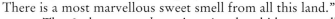

There is a most marvellous sweet smell from all this land."

The 2nd century *bc* writer Agatharchides marvelled that: "The sense of wonder transcends the sheer pleasure of the aromatic products, which are stored and aged, or even the creative force that nourishes them; most awesome of all is the flourishing of a fully divine and mature exhalation of wondrous perfume."

INCENSE BURNER SHOWING A CAMEL RIDER
c. 3rd century ad
From Shabwa
Calcite-alabaster
Presented by H. St J.B. Philby (1885-1960)

This incense burner was acquired in 1936, at the ancient city site of Shabwa by the famous Arabian traveler and explorer H. St. J.B. Philby. The two line Sabaean inscription implies that it was dedicated to a temple by "Adhlal, son of Wahabil." This individual is possibly the same as that shown on the front, that is, a man seated in front of the hump of a dromedary camel (Camelus dromedarius), with a circular shield or a waterskin slung above the camel's left rear leg. This style of camel riding is also illustrated on north Arabian Desert graffiti. The dromedary is indigenous to Arabia but, although hunted as a source of meat, was not domesticated until the early 1st millennium *bc*. This development greatly increased the value of camels, not only as a new source of transport but also as a valuable source of milk and hair, important secondary products that came to economically outweigh the value of these animals as a potential source of meat.

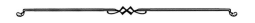

The Early Islamic author Marzuqi claimed that, prior to the Islamic Conquest in the 7th century *ad*, Yemeni perfume manufacturers had been so skilled that Indian traders arranged to supply the raw ingredients and then export the finished products back to their own country. Likewise, during that period, South Arabian perfumes are said to have been supplied to both the Persian and Byzantine Courts. However, it is not clear what containers were used to store or export perfume from South Arabia, whereas the equivalent incense industry has left considerably more identifiable remains in the archaeological record.

The frequency and variety of shape and size of the incense burners found within this region underline the importance of incense within local society, which is a feature that continues today, and in the colorful bazaars of Yemen you can still find many different types of frankincense for sale. Stone and pottery incense burners are the most commonly surviving types, whereas although metal incense burners were doubtless the most valuable they do not survive in great numbers, probably because the metal was recycled once the object was discarded. Different types may have been preferred for different functions as cuboid incense burners were preferred for personal use, and those of pyriform shape were used in temples. The concentration of examples in excavated gateway contexts at Timna and Sumhuram (modern Khawr Ruri) has been interpreted as possible evidence for gateway rituals. The shallow recessed upper portion held the incense and varied in form, whereas the fronts were often decorated with divine astral symbols, the stone incense burners were occasionally also inscribed with the names of one or more varieties of incense, and a total of thirteen types are now attested in this manner.

According to classical writers, the most valuable form of incense in the Mediterranean was frankincense and myrrh, and for the same reason these were listed in the Gospels (Matthew 2:1-11) among the presents offered by the Magi to the newborn Christ. Frankincense (also known as olibanum from the Sabaean term libnay via the Greek libanos and Latin libanum), is an oleo-gum-resin obtained from several species of tree called Boswellia. These grow up to 8 or 10 m. in height, have a peeling papery bark, and prefer dry rocky locations such as stony cliffsides. Several varieties of this species grow in the Dhofar and eastern Hadramawt regions of Southern Arabia, as well as parts of tropical and northeastern Africa, Soqotra and India. The African regions were the nearest and perhaps most conveniently situated to supply ancient Egypt, and as frankincense trees are depicted on reliefs in the temple of the Egyptian Queen Hatshepsut (1583-1402) at Deir el-Bahari, it has been variously argued that the famed land of Punt to which Hatshepsut and other Egyptian rulers sent periodic expeditions, was situated somewhere in eastern Sudan, Ethiopia or Somalia. However, at least by the 5th century *bc*, it appears that Southern Arabia had become the major exporter of incense

Although Theophrastus of Eresos, a Greek writer of the 3rd century *bc*, wrote that incense trees were cultivated in this region, this is more likely to be a misunderstanding of the fact that the gum is extracted by cutting the bark of wild trees between the months of May and December, and regularly collecting the tear-shaped globules of oozing milky white gum which gradually dries to a pale yellow or yellowish-brown color. This process was accurately described by the later Classical writer Pliny the Elder (*ad* 23-79), although he never saw it first-hand:

> "It used to be the custom, when there were fewer opportunities of selling frankincense, to gather it only once a year, but at the present day trade introduces a second harvesting. The early and natural gathering takes place at about the rising of the Dog-Star [Sirius], when the summer heat is most intense. They make an incision where the bark appears fullest of juice and distended to its thinnest; and the bark is loosened with a blow, but not removed. From this incision a greasy foam spurts out, which coagulates and thickens, being received on a mat of palm-leaves where the nature of the ground requires this, but in other places on a space round the tree that has been rammed hard. The frankincense collected in the latter way is in a purer state, but the former method produced a heavier weight; while the residue adhering to the tree is scraped off with an iron tool, and consequently contains fragments of bark."

Pliny also details how the frankincense collected in the autumn from the summer crop was "the purest kind, bright white in color" and was called carfiathum, from the South Arabian kharif, whereas the second crop harvested in spring "is reddish" and was called dathiathum, from the South Arabian datha. This custom of double cutting enabled the twice yearly shipments of the dried resin to the port at Qana and/or overland to Shabwa. Frankincense bark was also valued as an aromatic: the best quality was described by Dioscorides as being "thick, fat, fragrant, new, smooth and neither coarse nor thin," and in Yemeni bazaars it is currently more expensive than frankincense itself.

Myrrh is a similar translucent yellow resin which derives from Commiphora myrrha, one of almost two hundred species of the Commiphora genus known from Africa to India. C. Myrrha is a thorny multi-stemmed shrub or small tree growing up to 4 m. in height, which is found in eastern Ethiopia, parts of Somalia and in Yemen, mainly south of a line stretching from Marib to Shabwa. The ancient uses for myrrh were many, ranging from oil, a bitter additive to olive oil and wine, a medicinal balm and an ingredient in the perfume and Egyptian mummification industries. It is still used in Yemen to improve bad breath.

Several other aromatic plants were used in and exported from ancient South Arabia. These included cassia, and ladan or gum labdanum, which is a sticky oleoresin derived from a scrubby bush in the Cistus family. It burns with a bright flame and strong sweet smell, and was also popular in perfume and medicine. In addition, the Roman authors failed to realize that a number of other items which were treated as Arabian products were in fact imports from India or further east. These included aloe and "dragon's blood" resins from Soqotra, cardamom, cumin and costus from India, and cinnamon bark from Sri Lanka, which was burnt as an aromatic and employed as an ingredient in perfume.

Reliable statistics on the actual volume of trade in these periods are impossible to reconstruct: calculations based on Pliny's figures suggest an exaggerated annual delivery of 1300 - 1700 tons of frankincense and 450 - 600 tons of myrrh, but it was sufficient for Pliny to sarcastically remark that: "And by the lowest reckoning India, China, and the Arabian peninsula take from our empire 100 million sesterces every year - that is the sum our luxuries and our women cost us."

The South Arabian merchants had therefore created and partly controlled a powerful export trade based on expensive and exotic aromatics which had become essential ingredients for the Court, temple, spice markets and perfume industries of the Near East and Mediterranean. The routes by which these luxuries reached Rome were two-fold. Pliny describes in detail how the:

> "Frankincense after being collected is conveyed to Shabwa [the capital of the Hadramawt] on camels...and a tithe estimated by measure and not by weight is taken by the priests...It can only be exported through the country of the Qatabanians, and accordingly a tax is paid on it to the king of that people as well. Their capital is Timna, which is 1487 miles distant from the town of Gaza in Judaea on the Mediterranean coast; the journey is divided into sixty-five stages with halts for camels. Fixed portions of the frankincense are also given to the priests and the king's secretaries, but besides these the guards and their attendants and the gatekeepers and servants also have their pickings. Indeed all along the route they keep on paying, at one place for water, at another for fodder, or the charges for lodging at the halts, and the various tolls. Hence expenses mount up to 688 denarii per camel before the Mediterranean coast is reached, and then again payment is made to the customs officers of our empire. Consequently the price of the best frankincense is six, of the second best five, and of the third best three denarii a pound...No tithes are given to a god from myrrh, as it also grows in other countries; however the growers have to pay a quarter of the yield to the king of the Qatabanians. For the rest it is brought up all over the district from the common people and packed into leather bags; and our perfumiers have no difficulty in distinguishing the different sorts by the evidence of the scent and consistency...The prices vary with the supply of buyers; that of myrrh oil ranges from three to fifty denarii a pound, whereas the top price for cultivated myrrh is eleven denarii."

Pliny's description illustrates how many people benefited economically, and how the camel as the proverbial "ship of the desert" was fundamental to the Arabian export trade. The date of domestication of the camel in Arabia is still debated by scholars but although there is evidence for camel bones at 3rd millennium *bc* sites in eastern Arabia, these may simply reflect the consumption of wild beasts hunted for their meat and hides. It is only within the late 2nd and early 1st millennia *bc* that the archaeological evidence for the use of camels as means of transport becomes certain. Palace reliefs from the palace of Assurbanipal (668-627 *bc*) at Nineveh (in northern Iraq), illustrate northern Arabian tribesmen fleeing Assyrian soldiers on camels, and an inscription left by the same king refers to how: "Camels like flocks I divided up and shared out to the people of Assur. Within my land one bought a camel at the market gate for a few pence."

The ability of the camel to carry heavy loads, go without water for up to a month in winter and several days even in the height of summer, and to forage on most unpromising of desert shrubs, made it an invaluable means of traversing the otherwise inhospitable deserts of Arabia. In so doing it, not only opened up new foreign markets but helped break the previous isolation of Southern Arabia.

The second important means of trade with Southern Arabia was via the Red Sea. The most evocative source for this is the Periplus of the Erythraean Sea, which was written in the mid-1st century *ad*, and which lists the ports and principal imports and exports from Egypt to Southern Arabia and beyond to East Africa and India. Underwater surveys in the harbor of the port of Qana indicate that there were no fixed harbor installations, and instead trade must have resembled the traditional pattern still to be seen in this region or on the East African coast, whereby the ships anchored offshore and relied on smaller craft to load and off-load. However, earlier still, the Egyptian pharaoh Hatshepsut (1583-1402 *bc*), is known to have sent

fleets to Punt, a region variously identified as somewhere in eastern Sudan, Ethiopia or Somalia on the opposite side of the Red Sea to Yemen, and from which an aromatic resin known in Egyptian as "ntyw" was imported. This has been translated as either myrrh or frankincense, but the realistic depictions in her temple at Deir el Bahari suggest the latter. According to the Old Testament, Solomon also "built ships at Ezion Geber, which is near Elath in Edom [in the Gulf of Aqaba] on the shore of the Red Sea. And Hiram [a Phoenician king] sent his men - sailors who knew the sea - to serve in the fleet with Solomon's men. They sailed to Ophir and brought back 420 talents [14.5 tons] of gold, which they delivered to Solomon" (1 Kings 9).

In addition, the Persian Emperor Darius I (521-486 *bc*), constructed an early version of the Suez canal to link the Nile with the Red Sea, in what must have been a deliberate attempt to maxmize the market potential of Red Sea trade. However the problems facing all these maritime ventures were the long stretches of waterless coast, treacherous currents and the different wind-systems which effectively cut the Red Sea into two zones at the...degree of latitude.

INSCRIBED UNGUENT JAR
3rd century bc - 1st century ad
Calcite-alabaster
Lent to The Bowers Museum by Mr. Jerry Graves

This container belongs to a class of so-called "beehive" shaped jars which date between the 3rd century *bc* and 1st century *ad*. Over seventy examples have been published, most of which have been found in southwest Arabia, but occasionally at sites in Saudi Arabia and the Persian Gulf, which were connected with the incense trade, and in one case even as far away as Nineveh in northern Iraq. Some of these containers have been found in temples, whereas others were found in private houses or graves. However, only one of these previously published jars was inscribed, in that case simply with the names of two individuals. In this case, however, the jar is inscribed on both sides. Previously, vessels of this distinctive shape have been interpreted as containers for perfumed oils, aromatic gum resins or semi-solid unguents (aromatic ointments) such as the "Balm of Gilead," which was described in the Bible as a particularly valuable commodity. The inscription on this jar now confirms that that these were indeed used in the incense trade, and that they may even be regarded as branded packaging for one of the most desirable commodities of ancient Arabia.

OVERSIZE STAMPS
1st-3rd centuries ad
Bronze
Purchased from Malcolm Hay & Geoffrey Turner

Cast copper alloy oversize stamps, with openwork South Arabian inscriptions of the names "HYN" and "HRN," with handles on the reverse. The function of stamps such as these was unclear until recently. Recent archaeological excavations at Qana and the Red Sea ports of Berenike and Myos Hormos have revealed large numbers of circular plaster bungs which had been used to seal pottery amphorae, prevent leakage and preserve the quality of the contents. In other cases, bungs of cork or chipped pottery sherds were used. In each case, these were cheap and easy to make, and thus were equally easily disposable. Most were plain but the plaster bungs were occasionally inscribed in ink, or impressed before drying with stamps such as this. The inscriptions designated the merchants and/or the origin of the contents, apparently in imitation of the Roman practice of sealing wine amphorae. The bronze stamps were, therefore, an integral part of the process of manufacture and trade of commodities in South Arabia, and examples of these impressed bungs have since been recognized at Hayd ibn Aqil, Marib, Baraqish and Qaryat al-Fau.

INCENSE BURNER WITH FIGURE OF AN IBEX OR
WILD GOAT (OVIS ORIENTALIA)
Possibly 3rd century bc
From Marib
Bronze
Presented by Dr. Sidney E. Croskery

This cast bronze incense burner is in the form of a bowl with a splayed foot, one wall raised to form a sort of shield surmounted by spikes, with the front decorated with the standing figure of an ibex or wild goat below star and crescent moon symbols, which were originally highlighted with inlay, now missing. Traces of the clay core resulting from the original lost-wax casting process are visible within the bowl. The animal presumably served both as a convenient handle and as a cult object. It was obtained by the donor while she worked in Yemen as a medical doctor (1939-1967). Two very similar bronze incense burners exist in the University Museum in Philadelphia, and the Metropolitan Museum of Art in New York, and others are reported from excavations at Timna. A similar ivory container was excavated in a 9th century *bc* context at the site of Hama in central Syria, and has been previously interpreted as an early South Arabian export to the Levant, but whether it was indeed made in Southern Arabia is uncertain, as is its function, because ivory is not a particularly suitable material for an incense burner.

Architecture

"All these cities are ruled by monarchs and are prosperous, being beautifully adorned with both temples and royal palaces"
(Strabo).

Ancient South Arabian cities and towns were generally irregular in plan but, after the 7th century *bc*, they were invariably enclosed within ashlar masonry curtain walls standing 8-15 m. high, and equipped with simple gateways and slightly projecting towers of the same height as the walls. The origins of these urban centers is unclear, but each of the capitals of the historical South Arabian kingdoms appear to begin in the late 2nd millennium *bc* and mark a shift in power from earlier centers of population in the highlands or on the southern coast at Sabr. They were usually known in South Arabian as Hagar, but the size of these cities varied from some 6 to 10 hectares. The capitals were significantly larger: Timna covered some 30 hectares, the walls of Shabwa enclosed some 57 hectares, and Marib covered 90 hectares. Marib was the largest ancient city in Southern Arabia, and thus was justly the only one to become famous outside the region. Within the walls the agglomeration of families belonging to the same tribe or clan may explain the apparently haphazard pattern of urban development, which distinguishes the so-called "Arabian city" from the preplanned orthogonal foundations of the ancient Near East or classical world. However, there were focal points which underline the dual importance of the market and the temple, and which hint at pre-Islamic origins for these features which characterize the later Muslim pilgrimage cities of Mecca and Medina. At the Qatabanian capital of Timna, excavations have shown that the center of the city was dominated by a

FRIEZE DECORATED WITH A FRUITED GRAPEVINE PATTERN
2nd century ad
Calcite-alabaster
From Marib
Purchased from Professor Robert Bertram Serjeant (1915-1993)

Fruited grapevine decoration was a particularly popular form of architectural decoration in the classical world: a similar style of decoration occurred, for instance, on the north portico of the 2nd century *ad* Sanctuary of Bel in the Syrian oasis-city of Palmyra. This form of decoration was occasionally also employed on portable items such as incense burners.

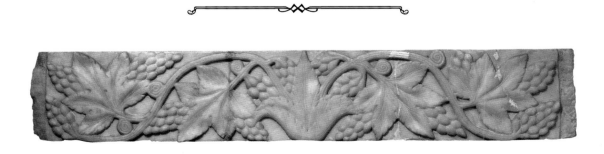

massive temple, with the principal marketplace situated in, and surrounded by, relatively large and carefully constructed houses.

The French archaeological excavations at Shabwa, which was capital of the Hadramawt between the 5th century *bc* and 5th century *ad*, have revealed more about the internal Organization of one of these cities. It was almost completely surrounded by a circle of low hills, upon which was built the outer fortification wall dating possibly to the 1st century *bc*, whereas an inner wall dated to the 7th or 6th century *bc*. Between these walls was an extensive salt dome, which offered a major source of revenue as salt was extensively traded and taxed in antiquity. The eastern part of the city was packed with large two-story houses, which also lined a major road connecting the Sayyin dhu-Alim temple with one of the north gates (and one of the likely entry points for the frankincense caravans which were the main source of the city's wealth). Immediately inside this gate lay the royal palace, which was known as Shaqar. This building was founded in the 10th or 9th century *bc*, although it was probably not a palace at this date; it was destroyed by a Sabaean army in *ad* 225, but then rebuilt a few years later as a timber framed porticoed structure. The ground floor was decorated with frescoes similar in style to wall paintings found in Roman Syria, and showing floral designs and men and women wearing classical dress; an upper floor contained hexagonal columns covered with carved vertical vine scrolls, and supporting double capitals showing classical style griffins. In addition, elaborate coffered ceilings were created with wooden boards, sometimes with red painted decoration, and thin alabaster panels.

Apart from this palace, a total of some 250 large houses have been identified. These had rectangular stone foundations, with walls up to 2 m. thick, reaching a height of 3-5 m. above the ground and supporting a superstructure constructed of wood and mud brick. The first floor was accessed via a staircase, which was built against the exterior of the foundation wall. Each of these buildings may have housed up to 15 people, giving a population estimate of up to 4,000 people living in such tower houses at Shabwa. These tower houses had the effect of enhancing security as each was easily defensible, and fostered the maintenance of an extended family within a single household, a feature which must also have had social implications. The survival of another 3rd or 4th century wall painting from this site, which shows one of these basement style South Arabian houses with two stories helps confirm the antiquity of one of the most distinctive features of Yemen, which is its traditional architecture, particularly the spectacular multistory houses of the Hadramawt which rise up to 20 m. in height.

South Arabian inscriptions provide further clues as to the appearance of certain types of public architecture, as the purpose of many was to commemorate the construction or repair of these buildings. One inscription from the site of Baynun in the Yemeni highlands, and dated to between *ad* 320-330, specifically refers to the construction of a palace five or more stories in height. Another refers to how one Muhabyah Atkan, son of Manakhum, "built, founded, prepared and completed the stonework of their house from the bottom to the top, six ceilings with six floors."

Pecked and marginally drafted ashlar masonry was a hallmark of monumental South Arabian architecture. The use of tall monolithic columns, often of stone, but also of wood, was another feature of the major buildings. Tall narrow multiple niches or so-called "false windows," were used as an architectural device to create a sharply contrasting pattern of light and shade not only on building facades, but also in miniature on architectural fittings. This created an identical effect to a characteristic feature of building facades in Urartian Anatolia and Achaemenid Iran, but although this is unlikely to be coincidence, it is uncertain how and when these influences arrived in Southern Arabia. The South Arabian collection in The British Museum includes a small number of pieces which provide hints at the architectural decor in some of the major public buildings. They are typically carved from limestone or calcite-alabaster: some are decorated with the traditional South Arabian pattern of a horizontal row of dentils projecting along the top and resembling a row of beam-ends, whereas others carry vine scroll or acanthus motifs borrowed from the classical world.

Unfortunately, no excavations have yet taken place within the ancient Sabaean capital at Marib, but the site of the palace and several temples are known, as are two important temple complexes outside the city walls, and which are known as the Awwam and Baran temples. It has been generally assumed that the oldest part of the city site lay beneath a prominent mound capped by a recent village but recent core drilling by a German archaeological expedition indicates that although there are 3rd millennium and early 2nd millennium layers, which have been dated by radiocarbon dates, most of this mound actually only dates from the 15th century and later.

Less is known about rural vernacular architecture, but unsurprisingly this was constructed according to local building traditions. The Hadramawt excavations at Raybun and al-Guraf have indicated the typical construction of two-story half-timbered mud brick buildings, with a single staircase connecting the two floors. Dry stone was the preferred building material in the Marib and Bayhan areas, and in the Wadi Surban, the earlier Bronze Age practice of constructing circular structures with flimsy roofs supported by a central pole was replaced between the 8th and 5th centuries *bc*, by one whereby rectangular houses were built with high stone basements supporting an upper floor.

The development of urbanism is normally closely tied to successful agricultural policies necessary for the sustenance of high populations. The oasis settlements of the desert fringe were totally reliant on irrigation agriculture based on the control of seasonal floods known in Arabic as *sayl*. The annual deposition of silt was beneficial in terms of soil fertility, but created a problem as the rise in the level of the fields meant that either the irrigation systems upstream had to be rebuilt or, in the case of Shabwa, huge efforts were made to clear away up to one meter of silt each year. The larger irrigation works relied on high level maintenance and inscriptions referring to their construction or repair are therefore fairly frequent. Surveys in the Wadi Surban have revealed traces of local irrigation works, but the most famous surviving evidence of ancient water engineering in Southern Arabia is the massive dam at Marib. This was constructed on the Wadi Dhana, some 7 km. upstream of the city of Marib. An earth barrage was constructed to hold the seasonal floods, which were diverted through a massive pair of stone sluices into channels capable of irrigating up to 10,000 hectares around the city. Until recently, these sluices had been regarded as possibly 6th century *bc* in date, based on inscriptions embedded within the walls. However, most of these inscriptions had simply been reused from earlier constructions elsewhere, and were held together with lead-coated iron clamps within a construction now demonstrated to have been constructed as late as the mid-5th or 6th century *ad*. This late dating raises further questions over the development of the Marib oasis in this period, as it was previously assumed to have been largely abandoned in favor of a highland capital; archaeological deposits of this period have not been recognized in the Awwam temple or adjoining cemetery, but this is probably connected with the increasing switch to the monotheistic religions of Judaism and Christianity. The final breaching of this dam in the late 6th century must have had a dramatic effect on the rural as well as the urban population of the oasis.

Within the Yemeni highlands, recent radiocarbon dates and landscape surveys indicate that the spectacular terraced fields which form one of the most distinctive features of the local landscape began in the Bronze Age. This is a very important discovery, as these systems are capable of supporting high populations, and unlike the dam based irrigation agriculture of the lowlands, is not susceptible to disastrous flooding, although they do require regular maintenance. They also significantly predate equivalent systems from the Levant which are believed to only originate in the 1st millennium *bc*, and demonstrate yet again the conservatism of tradition within Southern Arabia. Between the 1st century *bc* and 6th century *ad* the highlands became the center of the Himyarite state, and there was increased investment in water management systems with the construction of masonry dams designed to supplement the water supply and traditional reliance on terracing.

The engineered agriculture of Southern Arabia helped create a booming economy which could sustain higher populations than most other parts of Arabia. It is for this reason that the 1st century *bc* Roman historian Diodorus Siculus contrasted it with Jordan and enthused:

> "Now adjacent to this waterless and desolate land is another Arabia so much superior to the first that, from the great profusion of foodstuffs and other material goods produced therein, it has been named Arabia the Fortunate. For it brings forth reeds and rushes in abundance and every other aromatic shrub besides and, in general, all manner of fragrant foliage. And it is famous for the varied scents of the gummy exudations from its trees; for the most remote corner of this land produces myrrh, as well as frankincense, which is most pleasing to the gods and is exported to all the inhabited world. And such luxuriant pastures and thickets of costus and cassia grow here, as well as cinnamon and other such spices, that those commodities which in other lands are dedicated as rarities on the altars of the gods are among the Arabians mere kindling for their cooking pots."

FRAGMENTARY ARCHITECTURAL PEDIMENT
2nd century ad
Calcite-alabaster
From Marib
Purchased from Sotheby's

This fragment may have originally belonged to the same building as a well-known fragment of sculpture from Marib, and formerly in the Aden Museum (of which details are illustrated on modern Yemeni 20 and 100 rial banknotes). This depicts a nude female bust emerging from a vine spray and wearing a beaded necklace and armlets; this scene is set below a triangular pediment decorated with fruited grapevines, with a presumed pair of antithetical mythical beasts set in the corners above, of which The British Museum fragment would represent the right-hand piece; the position of these beasts corresponds to that often filled by winged victories in eastern Roman architecture. The original appearance of this mythical beast can be reconstructed on the basis of the larger second fragment as a lion or dog-headed animal with wings (as here), and a long curled fish tail which was grasped from behind by a nude youth holding an unsheathed sword in his right hand. A variety of winged monsters are represented in ancient South Arabian art, including griffins.

The iconography of this particular sculpture may be inspired by classical mythology, and similar marine creatures are depicted on clay counters from Palmyra, and a monumental temple basin at Baalbek, both in what was then Roman Syria. The goddess figure has again been interpreted in the light of Syrian classical architecture as the goddess Atargatis, but it is more likely that she represents a local South Arabian deity. A minor detail, which nevertheless appears to be very unusual on ancient South Arabian sculptures, is that traces of a bright red pigment survive within the gaping mouth of the monster on this fragment. Scientific analysis reveals this to be mercuric sulphide, which in its natural state is generally known as cinnabar, while synthetic mercuric sulphide produced for use as a pigment is known as vermilion. Cinnabar is found naturally over much of the world, and is known to have been used as a pigment from the 2nd millennium *bc* in China, and is mentioned in the 1st century *ad* Periplus as being "produced in the island [of Soqotra], [where it was] collected from the trees [drop by] drop." This implies that South Arabian craftsmen occasionally employed bright pigments to highlight details on carved sculpture, but unlike their counterparts in Egypt, the Near East or in the classical world, they do not appear to have made very extensive use of pigment, and instead apparently relied on the effect of the strong natural light on the carved detail and natural beauty of the calcite-alabaster.

SABAEAN INSCRIPTION REFERRING TO IRRIGATION
2nd century bc
Limestone
Purchased from Charles Albert Brenchley through George Hallett

The four line Sabaean inscription on the face of this yellow limestone block reads: "Lahayathat Satran, Great Man of Faysan has constructed and founded and covered the two aqueducts of the three terraces for the two palm groves Matran and Mawharah. By Athtar and Almaqah."

This carefully cut inscription commemorates the construction by one Lahayathat Satran of a pair of gravity flow waterworks, which were apparently designed to irrigate adjacent palm groves belonging to the two named individuals, Matran and Mawharah. It also acknowledges the divine protection of the gods Athtar and Almaqah as a means of ensuring that the construction (and therefore the produce of the palm groves) will not be harmed. These two deities were often invoked together in offerings connected with the fertility of irrigated lands dedicated to the temple, and particularly at Marib.

Irrigation formed a fundamental basis of the agricultural economy of ancient Southern Arabia and reached its most spectacular level of development with the construction of the famous dam at Marib. The origins of this lie in the 6th century *bc* with the construction and periodic repair after floods of an earth dam measuring some 620 m. in length and 8 m. in height, which enabled an 8 km. long reservoir within the gorge of the Wadi al-Sudd behind. Annual flooding led not only to increasing damage of the dam, but also to a massive buildup of coarse sediment within the reservoir. The solution was to build a pair of massive stone sluices, which diverted the flood water through spillways and distributor canals into so-called northern and southern oases, later described in the Koran as "a garden on their left and a garden on their right," where the fields were flooded to a depth of up to half a meter and ensured two crops per year. The destruction of these sluices in the late 6th century *ad* led to the collapse of the irrigated field systems supporting the former Sabaean capital, and triggered an abandonment of this city. This event was later seized upon in the Koran as evidence for divine retribution for the pagan beliefs of the inhabitants of Saba (34:16-17), and was even described in one medieval story as the direct result of "red rats, as fat as porcupines but much stronger, gnawing at the wooden beams shoring up the dam" (Abu Mohammed ibn Abdallah al-Kisai, c. 1100).

Hitherto, the dam at Marib has been regarded as one of the great architectural achievements of the Sabaean state, and even dated as early as the 6th century *bc* on the basis of dated inscriptions. However, excavations as part of a reconstruction project conducted as recently as 2002 have provided dramatically different evidence for the date of this structure. It now appears that the early inscriptions were simply reused in later construction following two disastrous breaches of the dam in 454 and 455 *ad*. The dam, or at least the northern sluice, was completely rebuilt by the Sabaean king Shurahbil Yafur, who is said to have employed a workforce of 20,000 men for this purpose. The building inscription itself refers to the logistics of feeding this number of men as they are said to have required "285,340 measures of fine flour, milled wheat, barley, corn and dates; 1363 slaughter camels, sheep and cattle; 1000 pairs of oxen and 670 camels carrying drink of different types of grapes and 42 loads of honey and butter." A pair of second inscriptions record further monumental repairs and new construction by King Abreha in *ad* 548 but the entire system was finally abandoned when rising sedimentation blocked the canal and distributor and prevented the floodwaters from reaching the fields beyond.

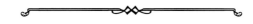

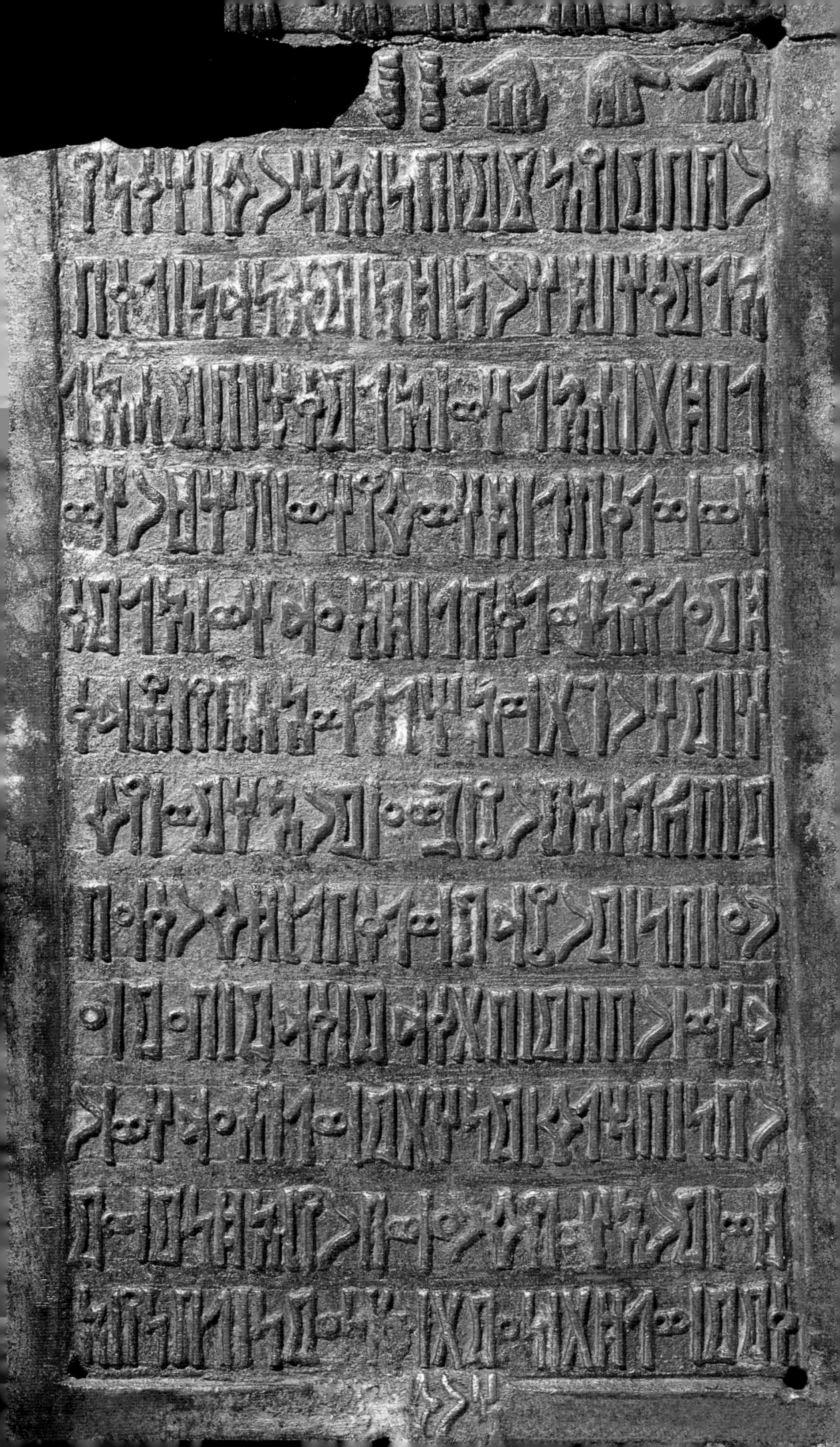

Language and Writing

"Immediately after this place and contiguous with it is the land of Arabia, for most of its length stretching along the Erythraean Sea. Different tribes inhabit it, differing in speech [from each other], some partly, others completely"
(*Periplus*).

The ancient kingdoms of Southern Arabia used an alphabetic script to write inscriptions in each of the four South Arabian dialects or languages of Sabaean, Qatabanian, Minaean (or Madhabian) and Hadramitic. These all belong to a family sometimes termed Sayhadic. The relative chronology of the different dialects is uncertain, but their popularity was partly related to the political success of the kingdoms in which they were predominantly spoken. Sabaean and Minaean appear to have been the oldest, and are attested from at least the 8th century *bc*; Sabaean was later adopted by the Himyarite rulers who unified Yemen in the late 3rd and early 4th century's *ad*, and thus survived the longest. Incidentally, 19th century publications typically refer to all South Arabian inscriptions as being Himyarite. Qatabanian was the dialect of the region of Qataban, which was centered on the Wadis Bayhan and Harib, but it was not widely used after the destruction of its capital at Timna in the 1st century *ad*. Finally, Hadramitic was the dialect of the Hadramawt, where it was established by the mid-1st millennium *bc* but it disappeared at the beginning of the 4th century *ad* when it was absorbed into Himyar.

The origins of the South Arabian Epigraphic or so-called musnad script, and the exact date at which it was developed, are still shrouded in uncertainty yet several features are clear. It consisted of 29 consonantal letters which survive in the Ethiopian syllabary, as opposed to the 22 letters of the Phoenician alphabet and from which the Greek alphabet was later derived. Some signs are identical or are closely related in the South Arabian

INSCRIBED PLAQUE MENTIONING A BATTLE BETWEEN THE SABAEANS AND THE ARABS IN THE JAWF
1st century bc-3rd century ad
Bronze
From Amran
Presented by Brigadier-General William Marcus Coghlan

This text is one of a large group of inscribed bronze plaques, which were originally attached to the walls or pillars of one or more buildings, probably temples, either below or close to the modern Yemeni highland town of Amran. The text was written by a local Sabaean, and not only illustrates the uneasy state of relations between Saba and the Arabs of the Jawf, but is the earliest preserved explicit description of a battle between them. The Arabs are known to have migrated into Yemen during the 1st and 2nd century's *ad*, creating a friction recorded in a number of inscriptions between these pastoral nomads and the existing settled South Arabian communities. The Sabaean inscription on this plaque reads:

> "Rabib Yazam of the tribe Akhraf has dedicated this inscription to Almaqah of Hirran, because Almaqah has demanded [it] from him in His oracle, and because he has kept him safe in his pilgrimage to dhu-Malasan, and because Almaqah has granted him trophies, spoils and captives, such as is right, on all occasions in which he paid service to his Lord Yafra ibn Marathid, and because He has saved his servant Rabib in the battle in which he faced the Arabs in the region of Manhat [modern Hizmat Abi Thawr]; and He may grant him the goodwill of his lord Yafra and the health of [his] mental and physical capacities, [and he has dedicated] for that which was favorable for the Banu Akhraf, and will be."

The top of the plaque is decorated with a row of hands which may have served an apotropaic function, and thus were intended to protect the inscription from bad fortune; alternatively they have been suggested to represent a "trophy" of the defeated Arabs mentioned in the inscription.

and Phoenician alphabets but it is unclear exactly how and when this may have occurred. However, the relative simplicity of alphabetic scripts over the complicated hieroglyphic or cuneiform writing systems of Egypt and the rest of the ancient Near East provides a clue in their wider adoption and eventual replacement. Vowels have been added in the various translated inscriptions included in this catalogue, but as these were not indicated in the original inscriptions it is not known exactly how many of the words were pronounced.

The inscriptions were written in four types of script. The earliest or archaic inscriptions represent personal names which were simply scratched or painted on pottery vessels, of which a small number have been excavated at the sites of Yala and Raybun, and dating between the 13th-12th and late 8th-early 7th centuries *bc*. Monumental inscriptions appear in the 7th century *bc*. These were very carefully carved using a highly geometric script, typically incised but occasionally carved in relief, whose similarity to early Greek inscriptions of the 6th and 5th centuries *bc* led initially to the argument that the two must be connected. These inscriptions were read in alternating directions from right to left, and left to right that is a style known by the Greek term boustrophedon from the custom of ploughing fields in similarly alternating directions. Later monumental inscriptions were simply read from right to left. The other scripts were a more baroque style used from the early 4th century *ad* with the letters carved in relief, and a minute, so-called minuscule, script which was incised on wooden sticks and which are a category of inscription only discovered in the 1970s. Comparison of the shapes and proportions of the inscribed letters offers a rough means of so-called palaeographic dating, but this is not very reliable as the same rules do not apply to all scripts or dialects.

The content of the South Arabian inscriptions has been understood since their discovery and publication in the 1860s and 1870s. They consist of four broad categories, namely formulaic religious texts concerning dedications and ritual acts; property claims dealing with the construction of or ownership rights to houses, walls, irrigation systems; commemorative texts dealing with particular military campaigns or monumental building projects; and prescriptive texts, mainly decrees concerning commerce, the division of land, and the regulation of irrigation, etc. The official inscriptions tend to be heavily stereotyped, but a wider vocabulary was employed on the sticks. The monumental inscriptions were usually on one or more rectangular blocks which were set side by side in the facade of the buildings in question. However, owing to regular recycling of stone for later construction, and the vagaries of acquisition, those inscriptions of this type which are found in museum collections, only tend to be isolated blocks and are therefore incomplete and not always easy to interpret. Many ancient graffiti also survive, although these are usually more difficult to read and have attracted less academic attention.

Finally, several thousand small inscribed sticks have now been discovered, although only thirty or so have so far been fully published. The sticks were made of ribs of date palm or Zizyphus spina Christi, measure between 10-30 cm. long, 2-5 cm. across, and are covered with up to fifteen lines of inscriptions incised in a cursive minuscule or so-called zabur script which was written lengthwise from right to left. Most are believed to come from the site of as-Sawda (the ancient city of Nashshan) in northern Yemen where they are believed to have formed the archives of the temple of the god Athtar. This confirms the information suggested by previously known stone inscriptions which indicated that royal edicts were inscribed twice, firstly as publicly visible monumental stone inscriptions and secondly on wooden sticks which were filed as archive copies. A small number of these sticks have also been excavated in a domestic area and temple of the goddess dhat-Himyam at Raybun in the western Hadramawt and dated between the 6th-1st centuries *bc*, indicating that these were once widely used in this region but have not normally survived. One of these reads as follows: "Haff, father-in-law [OR brother-in-law] of Wash...cried and disturbed her comfort. ... She manifested her goodwill and her forgiveness. He wrote down a draft and inscribed a stick because of his two wicked acts."

These inscribed sticks should revolutionize our understanding of life in ancient South Arabia, as they contain a wealth of information about subjects which are simply not covered by the monumental stone inscriptions. Those which have been published include private and business letters, including one which may be translated as: "To Shifinim from Urazan. May Athtar grant you well-being. The letter you wrote through Rahibum has arrived and has satisfied [us]. Now all your clients wish you well without end. And behold, send from Sanaa the contract [OR letter] of your daughter(s), so that Rahibum can meet them, when he comes from Zafar. And take it to heart to write [to] them again. Send regards to Hanium and send regards to Alhan, and may well-being be upon them."

Other documents consist of accounts, guarantees, school exercises and lists of names of tribes, soldiers and even women's names. They also confirm the drafting of contracts and other documents by professional scribes, although the social status of these within the predominantly illiterate society is unknown.

LARGE INSCRIBED PLAQUE
1st century bc-3rd century ad
Bronze
From Amran
Presented by Brigadier-General William Marcus Coghlan (1803-1885)

The frequency with which these plaques were used in antiquity is not only demonstrated by the large number which survive, but also by the attachment holes and iron nails found in situ on the facades and pillars of public buildings such as the Awwam temple at Marib. Very few have been found in archaeological contexts, and those reportedly found at Amran are believed to date between the 1st century *bc* and 3rd century *ad*, although palaeographic dating suggests a date as early as the 5th century *bc* for a similar example dedicated to Almaqah, and excavated near the peristyle hall of the Awwam Temple at Marib. These inscriptions were made not by simply casting in an incised mold, but instead made use of the so-called "lost wax technique," whereby the individual letters were formed by adding, trimming and punching where necessary separate threads of wax between incised lines on the face of a thick wax plaque which was then covered in several layers of clay, baked with molten bronze poured in through the side to replace the wax, before cracking off the clay shell and polishing the metal.

The incurved edges reflect shrinking of the wax original. The essentially rectangular shape with the flat raised frame around the recessed page indicates that they were influenced by the shape of hinged wooden or ivory writing boards where the inscriptions were incised into wax filled pages, the raised borders of which prevented the contents from smudging when the pages were folded together. This form of writing board was widely used throughout the Near East from at least the 14th century: the earliest example to survive is an ivory-hinged example found on the site of a shipwreck at Ulu Burun off southwest Turkey. Clay sealings of the same period which were excavated at the Hittite capital of Hattusha are believed to have originally been attached to similar wooden writing boards, and these boards are illustrated on 8th century Late Assyrian reliefs as well as being described in contemporary texts as being used alongside parchment scrolls and clay tablets. Mesopotamian texts refer to the beeswax on these boards being colored yellow with orpiment, which appears to have been a practical device of rendering the incised wax inscription easier to read in the sun; equivalent Roman scribes who continued to use writing-boards colored the wax with crushed charcoal.

This bronze plaque was among a collection of 26 inscriptions presented to the Museum in 1862, by Colonel (later Brigadier-General) William Marcus Coghlan (1803-1885), who was then serving as the East India Company Political Resident and Commandant in Aden. However, as early as about 1870, a Jew in Sanaa appears to have been making fake bronze inscriptions, but these are technically easily distinguishable from the originals, as they were cast in sand rather than clay (and therefore have a rougher finish), the lines are separated by raised lines (as on the stone inscriptions), the letters are not individually modeled, and the inscriptions themselves do not make sense. It is indicative that although the decipherment of the South Arabian script was still in its very infancy, questions were raised over the authenticity of these other plaques in correspondence between Samuel Birch (1813-1885), then newly appointed Keeper in the Museum's former Department of Oriental Antiquities, and Captain W.F. Prideaux (1840-1914) and Reverend Charles Kirk, the East India Company chaplain in Aden.

Religion

"I have just seen things unknown to you. With truthful news I come to you from Sheba, where I found a woman reigning over the people. She is possessed of every virtue and has a splendid throne. I found that she and her subjects worship the sun instead of God. Satan has seduced them and debarred them from the right path" (Koran 27:22-26).

The purpose of this Muslim reference was to indicate how the Queen of Sheba was a heathen, yet its reference to sun worship was not only wrong, but simplistic, as ancient Southern Arabia had a highly developed religious pantheon of over a hundred different deities. The importance of religion has long been evident, owing to the large number of surviving monumental stone inscriptions referring to temple dedications or invocations of the names of a wide variety of deities. On the basis of these, scholars from the second half of the 19th century onward have attempted to reconstruct the pantheon and the respective attributes of particular deities, although these are not without controversy, as texts specifically describing temple rituals are totally lacking, there are no definite depictions of deities, and Classical or later Arab sources were at best uninformed, as the passage above illustrates.

The most important deities mentioned in early South Arabian inscriptions were Athtar (a male version of the Babylonian Ishtar, described as a vengeful "God of Thunder" who was invoked against desecrators of graves and whose association with storms led to him being invoked during the course of rain inducing ritual ibex hunts); Hawbas (variously described as male, or a female counterpart to Almaqah); Almaqah (a form of national Sabaean deity who was god of agriculture and irrigation); and the two goddesses dhat-Himyam and dhat-Badanum. These were supplemented by dozens of other gods and goddesses, some of whom appear to have been restricted to individual tribes or towns and who may have been normally worshipped at small sanctuaries and household shrines rather than at major temples. The complexity of the pantheon thus underlines the heterogeneous character as well as the lengthy development of ancient South Arabian society.

INSCRIBED HAND DEDICATED TO THE GOD TALAB
2nd-3rd century ad
Bronze
Purchased from Spink & Son

The right hand is traditionally regarded as a powerful symbol of good fortune, and thus was widely illustrated in ancient South Arabia as an apotropaic motif on dedicatory inscriptions and, indeed, emphasized as a gesture of worshippers in their dedicatory statues and stelae. The same function probably explains a small number of bronze and plaster model hands (minus inscriptions) in other collections. The form of dedicatory inscription on this object is typical of bronze inscriptions, yet this is the first example to be discovered on part of the body, a practice that is nevertheless attested in South Arabian inscriptions. This hand was dedicated to the god Talab Riyam in a place called Zafar, although this appears to be different than the later Himyarite capital of the same name in the Yemeni highlands. The inscription reads: "Wahab Talab, son of Hisam, the Yursamite, subject of the Banu Sukhaym, has dedicated to their patron Talab Riyam [this] right hand, in his memorial dhu-Qabrat in the city of Zafar, for his well-being."

Its provenance is unknown, but it is said to have been first offered for sale by a sheikh from the Sanaa region to a British engineer working in Yemen. The inscription suggests that it may have originally been placed in a sanctuary belonging to a tribe believed to be from the Yemeni highlands north of Sanaa. The hand is very realistic, and may have been modeled on an actual hand, perhaps even of the dedicant himself. Scientific analysis indicates that this object was made of leaded bronze, containing some traces of silver and nickel. The object was cast using copper chaplets to hold the core, most of which was subsequently removed, although sufficient remained for thermoluminescence testing to confirm the purported age of the piece. The remains of two casting sprues are present at the wrist which indicates, firstly, that the metal was poured into the mold with the fingers pointing downwards and, secondly, that this is not a piece broken from a larger casting. There is evidence of work done on the surface after casting, including the addition of the inscription, which partly cuts a chaplet.

During the 1920s, it was proposed that most of these deities were no more than different manifestations of an astral triad of the sun, moon and Venus-star. Following this, attempts were made to equate particular deities with these bodies, such as Athtar with the morning star, Almaqah, Talab and Wadd with the moon, and Shamsun, Sayyin, dhat-Himyam and dhat-Badanum with the sun. However, this hypothesis, which was based on the depiction of astral symbols next to the names of deities on monumental inscriptions, is no longer generally accepted, nor is there any evidence that the South Arabian priests developed the sophisticated form of astronomical observations that earlier priests had in Mesopotamia. Other attempts have been made to equate particular animal motifs with specific deities, notably the bull, ibex and vine with Almaqah, the bull and gazelle with Athtar, the bull and eagle with Sayyin, the eagle with Nasr and Wadd, the horse and lion with dhat-Badanum, and the snake with Sahar and Nahasab. These attempts are also controversial: some of these motifs may have been apotropaic and this may better explain the repetition of motifs as framing devices, or their placement on functions as varied as funerary stelae from Qataban, and architectural gutters on Sabaean temples or the royal castle at Shabwa in the Hadramawt.

Each kingdom had a principal deity, with Almaqah assuming this role from Hawbas in the kingdom of Saba. In contrast, the chief god of the kingdom of Main, based at Qarnaw in the Jawf, was Wadd, although Nakrah was also worshipped here, and at the city of Baraqish where a massive temple dedicated to him has been excavated. In Qataban, the leading deity was Amm; hence Qatabanian inscriptions often refer to individuals as "children of Amm" (whereas Sabaeans are "children of Almaqah," etc). Finally, in the Hadramawt, the main god was Sayyin, who has previously been mistakenly equated with the Semitic moon-god Sin. Sanctuaries dedicated to Sayyin have been identified at several sites in this region, including Huraydah and Shabwa, in the latter instance approached by a monumental causeway.

The most famous of the surviving (although only partially excavated) South Arabian temples are the mighty Awwam temple. This was dedicated to the god Almaqah, lay a short distance south of the Sabaean capital at Marib, and consisted of an oval enclosure wall and surrounding complex, now choked in windblown sand, and which was known in Arabic as the Mahram Bilqis. It was apparently founded by the 9th century *bc*, if not earlier, and consists of an oval ashlar masonry enclosure wall measuring up to 260 m. across, with an inscribed facade standing over 16 m. high; access into the enclosure was through a massive columned peristyle hall on the northern side. The Awwam temple was a center of annual pilgrimage during the summer month of Abhi, and facilitated by its connection with the city by a processional road; regular provisions against the admission of women in an "impure" or menstrual state suggest that a wide degree of public access was otherwise permitted, and the sacrifice of livestock followed by ritual meals are also attested. Other pilgrimage centers included the temple of Sayyin dhu-Alim at Shabwa and a temple of Almaqah at Amran, whence a large number of inscribed bronze plaques derive. One 3rd century inscription describes when and how the pilgrimage to the sanctuary of the god Talab at the highland site of Riyam should be conducted, how many animals should be slaughtered, and what exactly should be done. The importance of pilgrimage extended to central and northern Arabia, and continued after the introduction of Islam with the creation of the fundamental hajj pilgrimage to the Muslim cities of Mecca and Medina.

The appearance of other ancient temples in South Arabia varied. The earliest identified, and one of the best preserved excavated religious structures, consists of a square building with a blank exterior which was dedicated to Athtar dhu-Risaf at as-Sawda (the ancient city of Nashshan) in the Jawf and dates to the 8th-7th centuries *bc*. This measured up to 50 m. across and consisted of a small paved inner courtyard surrounded by porticoes with a massive platform at one end, and entered from the outside through a passage with a narrow gate at each end decorated with incised scenes on the uprights of the doorways, with an imposing row of ten tall plain stelae outside. Similar engraved scenes showing figures in long gowns and holding curved swords or wands, and occasionally framed by rows of ibexes - a recurrent later design motif in South Arabian architecture - are found on the entrances of several other early temples in the Jawf at Haram, Kamna and Main.

However, during approximately the 6th-5th centuries *bc*, a new style of temple began to be constructed from the Jawf to Raybun in the Hadramawt. These favored stepped porticoed entrances and dark hypostyle court interiors containing benches and libation drains with a row of cellae with fixed doors at one end, and roofed with stone slabs supported on wooden columns. One temple at Raybun was dedicated to Rahban, and was found to be floored with woven palm-leaf mats with cloth drapes on the altars and decorated with polychrome wall paintings depicting human figures, fish and plants. The regular provision of fixed incense burners suggests that there was a heady smell of smoldering aromatics inside these enclosed spaces, whereas the blankness of the exterior facades served to emphasize the necessity of entering and engaging with the deity within.

Little is known about the priesthood, although the titles of different ranks of priests are attested in the larger temples owned estates. The reconstruction of ritual within the temple themselves is largely reliant on the excavated architectural fittings. These suggest that the offering of liquid libations onto the tops of metal and stone altars which poured through animal-headed gutters into drains was an important component. The burning of aromatics was equally important, and the discovery of excavated animal bone remains from immediately outside the Awwam temple suggest either the offering of cooked meat offerings, or possibly the commemorative banquets described in some texts. The provision of regular dedications commemorated by inscriptions set within or on the walls or placed directly on the object, such as a statuette, was another fundamental feature of temple ritual. References to the offering of a single item of livestock such as a goat, ram or camel, hint at a source of the economic upkeep of the temple, and actual animal sacrifice is referred to in some inscriptions, for instance: "On this the king will slaughter a bull on the ninth day of the month." Other inscriptions dating approximately between the 8th-4th centuries *bc* refer to the dedication of individuals, but this indicates the offering of people to the service of the temple, rather than gory human sacrifice as previously suggested; later inscriptions of the so-called Middle Sabaean period refer to the dedication of a statue or statuette.

The purpose of these offerings was very varied. Some individuals acknowledged military success, whereas others were intended to ensure good health, or the protection of the individual's herds of camels or other live-stock, and thus their economic livelihood. One exceptional inscription dating to the 1st or 2nd century *ad*, was dedicated by a woman giving thanks for the successful birth of her grandchild. Other inscriptions were added on models representing parts of the anatomy, including phalli; inscriptions from the Mayfaan temple at Raybun commemorated the healing of eye and skin ailments, and a temple to Naqrah, the god of healing, was excavated at Baraqish. The outstretched right hand was regarded as a particularly potent symbol of protection, and therefore recurs not only as a gesture made by individuals on certain funerary stelae, but also occasionally as three-dimensional inscribed or plain models in bronze or plaster. The consultation of oracles and drawing of lots belong to the same tradition, whereby individuals would seek divine opinion and favor.

During the 4th century *ad* the old South Arabian religions came under intense pressure with the rise of particularly Judaism, and to a lesser extent, Christianity which was centered on the city of Najran in what is now southwest Saudi Arabia. The latest inscriptions to refer to ancient South Arabian deities are dated to *ad* 378 or 383. The conversion of the ruling and upper social classes therefore ensured the end of the practice of dedicating these monumental inscriptions, the maintenance of the major temples, and centers of pilgrimage, and presumably began to affect burial rites, although it is likely that the process of conversion was slower in the countryside.

STATUETTE OF A WARRIOR GOD
Probably 1st-3rd century ad
Bronze
Presented by Mrs. H.C. Gowan

This cast copper alloy statuette of a male figure in Roman military dress may be a representation of a warrior god. The figure is wearing what appears to be a three-layered pleated skirt, which is an imitation of Roman armor, with a cuirass and belt worn over a pleated tunic. The statue may have been an imitation of a statue of the Roman god of war, Mars, who is usually depicted with a crested helmet. The deity is holding a patera (a broad flat saucer or dish particularly used in pouring out libations at sacrifices) in his right hand, and the left hand probably originally held a spear or shield.

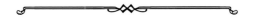

ALTAR WITH A SABAEAN DEDICATION
TO THE DEITY RAHMAW
Possibly 6th century bc
Tin-bronze
Possibly from Marib
Purchased from Christie's; said to have previously belonged
to Sharif Ahmed ibn Awadh al-Habili

This unique altar is one of the largest and most important examples of ancient South Arabian metal working. Its suggested date has been attributed on the basis of the palaeography (the shape of the letters). Two joining portions survive, the first and largest of which consists of the panel showing three rows of standing sphinxes shown frontally, set below a lightly projecting cornice around which runs the beginning of a Sabaean inscription. The raised letters were made by applying individual wax threads onto the panel before it was cast, and although most have been carefully smoothed, the uneven tops of some indicate how they were individually molded; the same technique was used to make the bronze dedicatory tablets. The second fragment represents the corresponding side of the altar, where the recessed top was drained by a pair of projecting bull's head gargoyles.

The altar carried a Sabaean inscription which commences on the most completely preserved portion, and has been translated by the Russian scholars A.G. Lundin and S. Frantsouzoff as:

"[...]il son of Ammanas, priest of Rahmaw, [has] dedicated to Rahmaw Lahayathat and Sabahhumaw when [he performed the h]unt of Athtar dhu-Musawwatim. By Ath[tar]…"

The name of the dedicant is unfortunately not preserved but the inscription has been interpreted as describing how the altar was dedicated to a local but previously unattested deity called Rahmaw, following the completion of a successful hunting trip. Successful hunting trips were believed to confer divine fortune, and even until recently in the Hadramawt it was said that "if we did not hunt, the rain would not come to us; there would be drought in the country and scarcity of food." However, this interpretation has since been challenged by the French philologist, C. Robin, and the inscription has been alternatively translated as follows: "[...]il son of Ammanas, priest of Rahmaw, [has] dedicated to Rahmaw Lahayathat and Sabahhumu, the day when he became minister of Athtar dhu-Musawwatim. By Ath[tar]…"

When the altar was first acquired, thick heavy corrosion products covered the surface to a depth of up to 5 cm. thick in places. After these were carefully removed, the inscription and decoration were made much more clearly visible, as were the "blow holes" resulting from the original casting, and the almost pure copper chaplets which had been used in antiquity to secure the core. Traces of burning mixed with the corrosion suggest that the temple in which the altar stood had been burnt or that it may have been discarded in a hot ashy deposit. Scientific analysis also indicated that the main part of the altar was probably made as a single casting from several separate melts poured successively into a mold; the metal composition is almost uniform with c. 11-14 % tin added to c. 83-90 % copper with the usual minor trace elements of lead, zinc, iron and nickel. Smaller fragments belonging to a second bronze altar also decorated with sphinxes, but made with a slightly different metal composition exist in The British Museum collection.

INSCRIBED BULL DEDICATED TO THE GODDESS DHAT-HIMYAM
1st-2nd century ad
Bronze
Purchased from Mr. Milligan

The Sabaean inscription reads: "to dhat-Himyam, two bulls," indicating that this was one of a pair of bull figures to be dedicated to this goddess. Scientific analysis confirms that this figure was cast from copper alloy and riveted onto the stepped base. The tail is broken, but was originally in an erect position. A very similar tin-bronze bull (minus an inscription) exists in the Metropolitan Museum of Art. Up to five others are known, and fragments of bronze and stone bull statuettes were also found in the Peristyle Hall of the Awwam temple at Marib. These frequent finds therefore indicate that they must have been a very popular form of dedication. The folds of skin around the neck and brow ridges are typical of South Arabian depictions of bulls and are also found on stone sculptures.

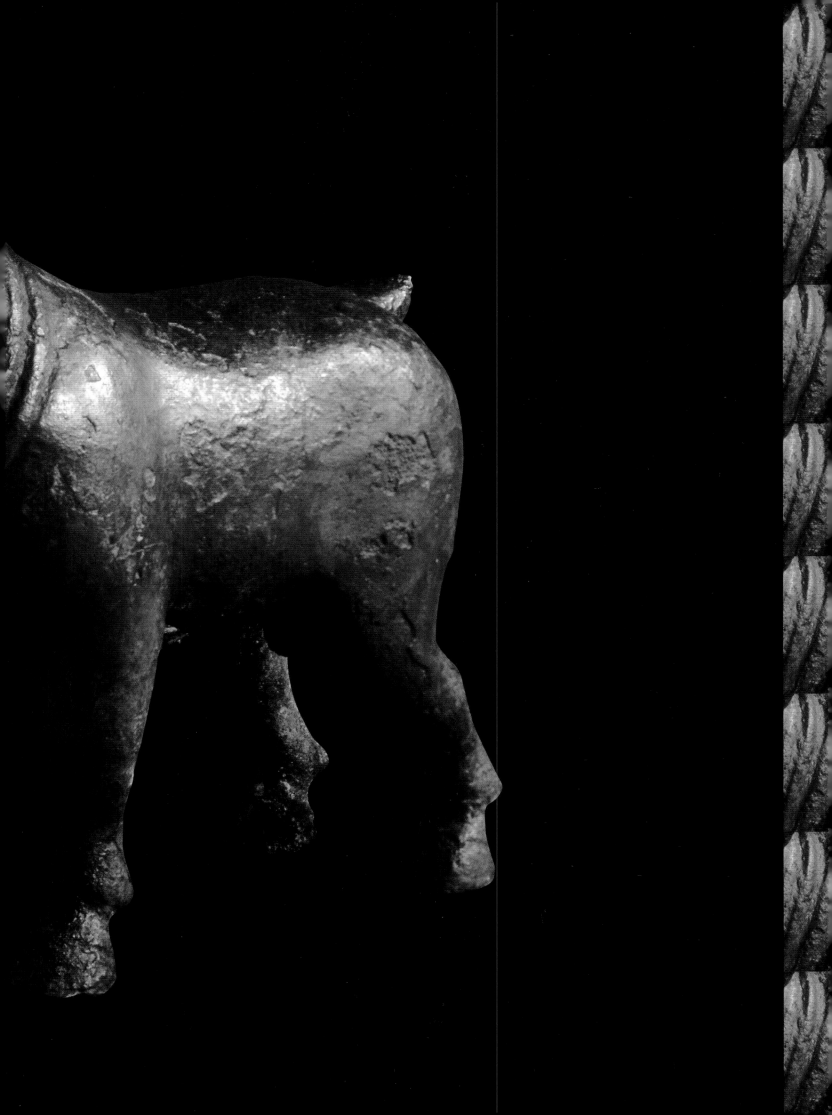

Metalwork

"Since they have never for ages suffered the ravages of war because of their secluded position, and since there is an abundance of both gold and silver in their country, especially in Saba, where the royal palace is situated, they have embossed goblets of every description, made of silver and gold, couches and tripods with silver feet, and every other furnishing of incredible costliness"
(Diodorus Siculus).

The origins of metallurgy lie in the Neolithic period of the Near East when early villagers began to experiment with the working of brightly colored and easily melted copper ores collected on the surface. Thus, over a hundred copper objects have been excavated at the 7th millennium *bc* site of Cayonu in southeast Turkey, where this material was particularly used for making beads, pins and awls. Lead followed as another easily malleable metal ore, and finally gold and silver began to be exploited in this region during the 4th millennium *bc* (although somewhat earlier in the Balkan region). By the Bronze Age metalworking had become a major industry throughout the Near East, not only near places where the ores occurred (notably Sinai, the Feinan

 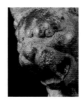 region of Jordan, Cyprus, Turkey, Iran and Oman), but also at far removed urban centers where concentrations of power and population ensured widespread demand by rulers, religious authorities and townsfolk alike. These urban metalsmiths were supplied by a flourishing trade and even royal gift exchange in bun shaped or "oxhide" ingots shipped by sea, river or canal, or carried overland by donkey or, from the late 2nd or 1st millennia *bc*, by camel.

The emergence of the Arabian camel caravan trade in the 1st millennium *bc* opened up new metal supplies to the traditional consumers of the Near East and Mediterranean. Gold, silver, lead and copper occur naturally in Southern Arabia, and had already provided rich resources for the local manufacture of statues, jewelry, vessels, weapons, tools and other items. However, whereas copper occurs widely in the Near East, gold does not, and it is effectively limited to gold bearing quartz veins in western and southern Arabia, Egypt and Nubia, or as

DECORATIVE FITTING WITH A SNARLING LYNX
1st-3rd century ad
Bronze
From Amran
Presented by Captain W.F. Prideaux (1840-1914)

This cast bronze fitting may have originally been attached to a piece of furniture. It is decorated with a snarling pouncing lynx, a motif which was borrowed from classical art. The back of the animal is decorated with a fruited grapevine, which is a classical motif introduced into Southern Arabia, and suggests that this object may date between the 1st and 3rd centuries *ad*. The object was apparently excavated at the town of Amran, and was described in 1873 by W.F. Prideaux in a seminal paper published in the Transactions of the Society for Biblical Archaeology, and entitled "On some recent discoveries in southwestern Arabia." The same town is the reported provenance for a large number of inscribed bronze plaques, and a small number of other metal objects presented to The British Museum in 1862 and 1863, and which appear to have been discovered here during construction in about 1855, but the town, now heavily rebuilt, has never been archaeologically investigated and the precise original context of these objects is unknown.

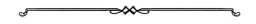

placer deposits in areas of western Turkey and Georgia. Given this distribution, and the southward trade connections of the kingdom of Israel, it is therefore not particularly surprising to find that I Kings: 10, associates the Queen of Sheba with this precious metal. It is perhaps a folk memory of this which survives in the famous legends of King Solomon's mines at Ophir, which continue to excite explorers and modern writers. The location of these has sometimes been sought in East Africa, particularly in Ethiopia, but western and southwest Arabia is a more likely source: Ophir is listed among the sons of Yoqtan in the book of Genesis (10:29), where it appears between Sheba (Southern Arabia), and Havilah (southern Palestine), and thus, if the genealogy matches geography, should be situated somewhere in western Arabia.

According to ancient Greek, Roman and Early Islamic authors, the sources of gold certainly extended from Yemen up the coast of western Arabia. In the 1st century *bc*, the Roman historian Diodorus Siculus wrote:

"Gold they discover in underground galleries, which have been formed by nature, and gather in abundance. It is not that which has been fused into artificial nuggets out of gold dust, but the virgin gold which is called, from its condition when found, 'unfired' gold ('for it is not smelted from ores, as is done among other peoples, but is dug out directly from the earth'). And as for size the smallest nugget found is about as large as a fruit stone and the largest not much smaller than a Persian walnut. This gold they wear about both their wrists and necks, perforating it and alternating it with transparent stones."

Geological surveys in western Arabia from the Medina region to the Maraziq area of the Jawf in northern Yemen, confirm the existence of extensive ancient and early medieval mines for gold and silver. The gold-workings followed quartz veins typically measuring 1-2 m. across and which occurred near eroded volcanic deposits. These are easily recognizable, as they are a brilliant white color against a darker rock, which explains how the ancient miners were able to find the sources. There is evidence for ancient surface test pits carried out to test the quality of the veins, as well as narrow deep mines measuring up to 150 m. in length. Actual mining tools have not yet been found, but this may be because they were too valuable to leave lying around, or simply because the miners used a combination of stone hammers and fire to crack the rock. The remains of old camps have been found close to the mines, with dry stone walls delimiting single or multi-room workshops, sometimes with the heavy stone tools still in place. These were made of deliberately selected hard stones which had been brought to the settlements, and included cubical hammers held with one or both hands, and used to pound lumps of ore placed on top of large stone anvils. Oval grinders typically measuring 50 x 25 cm. across were used to reduce the crushed fragments into a powder from which the gold dust could then be easily separated using water. The region is now rather barren, but the nearby streambeds suggest that there would have been sufficient water during the winter or spring not only for drinking, but also for the processing of the gold dust. This technology has close similarities with that used by the ancient Egyptians in Egypt and in Nubia, but it is not known whether this reflects the presence of Egyptian miners, or simply similarities in prospecting knowledge.

The earliest gold artifacts found so far in Yemen include a small number of beads excavated at the Bronze Age site of Sabr. Isolated items have been found at later sites, and a selection of simple earrings and chalcedony beads with decorated gold caps exist in the National Museum in Sanaa. The scarcity of surviving items of gold jewelry or indeed silver items is not surprising, as relatively few sites have been archaeologically excavated, many more have been severely looted in the past, and gold has always been subject to hoarding. The British Museum has one of the few collections of ancient South Arabian goldwork to survive, and which is said to have been found as a hoard concealed inside a reused softstone pot.

The date of the beginnings of metallurgy in this region are unknown, but the earliest metal objects dating from the early 3rd millennium *bc*, were excavated in tombs at Ruwaiq and Jabal Jidran, and consist of several pieces of copper alloy, including an awl. So far, metal objects have not been commonly found at settlement sites until the late 2nd-early1st millennium *bc*, when a range of unalloyed copper, low arsenical copper, and low tin-bronze axes, adzes, knives/daggers, awls, needles, fishhooks and rings have been excavated at sites in the Tihama and Lahj regions. Metallurgical slags found in one spot at the large coastal site of Sabr, imply local production but it is likely that finished items were also traded or exchanged between settlements. It is also significant that chipped stone, especially obsidian, continued to be extensively employed for making cutting tools well into the 1st millennium *bc*, implying that metal was still a material of prestige and high status. Small clay crucibles containing solidified traces of molten copper have been found at several late settlement sites, including Timna and Khawr Ruri, thus providing proof of metalworking in workshops at these settlements; and casting debris found near a funerary temple at Hayd ibn Aqil is believed to be from the manufacture of inscribed plaques. However, on survey, crucibles have not been found at mining settlements, suggesting that these last stages of metalworking were carefully controlled at or close to the centers of demand.

During the 1st millennium *bc*, the South Arabian metalsmiths extensively developed the use of the so-called "lost-wax" casting of bronze, to which in later centuries they added up to 9% of lead in order to enhance the fluidity of the molten metal. This casting technique involved the modeling of an original in wax, invariably on a clay core in the case of three-dimensional sculptures, encasing the model in clay, heating until the molten wax poured out filling the hollow with molten metal, allowing the mold to cool, before cracking off the clay surround and filing and polishing the cold metal. The result, was the production of a wide range of naturalistically modeled dedicatory statues and statuettes, ranging from the miniature to the over life-size, large inscribed measuring buckets or altars, incense burners and lamps, and inscribed plaques made in imitation of the pages of wooden writing boards, which were nailed up on temple walls.

The styles of the metal statuary in particular are very instructive. The earliest large example possibly dates to the 6th century *bc*, and famously depicts an individual named Madikarib, dressed in a wrap around skirt or kilt, with a straight dagger thrust through the belt, a lion skin draped across his shoulders, and a plumed headdress on his head. The relatively early date of this figure, which was excavated in the Awwam temple at Marib in 1951/52, and is part of the collections in the National Museum in Sanaa (Yemen), undermines the old view, that South Arabian culture was totally reliant on influences from the classical world. Instead, it is part of a wider preclassical local tradition of metalworking, which was also responsible for the production of many other, albeit less well preserved, statues found at the same site as well as the massive bronze altar in this exhibition. Later still, by the 1st and 2nd centuries *ad*, there is clearer evidence for the influence of Roman style on the depiction of drapery, and the adoption of mythological compositions, including possible representations of Dionysos or the divine twins, Castor and Pollux, as massive cast bronze sculptures found at Ghayman and Timna. In 1931, a pair of fragmentary larger than life-size bronze statues of King Dhamarali Yuhabirr and his son Tharan, shown as nude classical style heroes, were discovered at a Himyarite town-site at an-Naklat al-Hamra: significantly, inscriptions indicate that they were made by an artist with the Greek name of Phokas, and "assembled" by a local craftsman called Lahayamm, suggesting that they were cast using imported molds. Finally, the dramatic discovery in the last phase of the Sayyin temple at Shabwa, of the imprints for the hooves of four horses which were larger than the famous Roman horses at San Marco in Venice (which are the largest surviving castings from the classical world), and the 1 m. long imprints for the feet of a colossal human statue, proves the conspicuous consumption and ostentatious display of metal in ancient Southern Arabia.

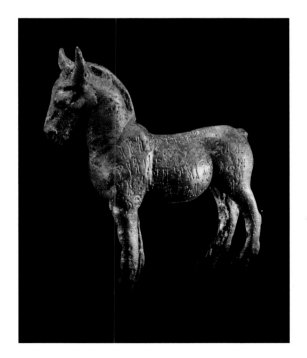

ASS OR DONKEY
WITH DEDICATORY INSCRIPTION
Possibly 2nd century ad
Bronze
Purchased from Spink & Son, Ltd.

This beautifully modeled statuette was cast using the lost wax process. It is inscribed with a four line inscription. Scientific examination indicates that this object was cast from a low tin-bronze, with little subsequent tooling, as is evidenced by the "flash" of metal between the forelegs; the inscription also appears to have been cast rather than added later.

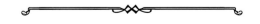

HEAD OF A MAN
Possibly 2nd century ad
Bronze
From Ghayman
Lent to The British Museum by Her Majesty the Queen, Elizabeth II

This exceptional piece was presented by Imam Yahya ibn Mohammad (ruler of northern Yemen from 1905-1948), to King George VI (1895-1952), on the occasion of his coronation on December 11, 1936. The site where it was found has not been properly investigated, but a number of other bronze objects have been reported from here, following unscientific excavations carried out before the Second World War. These were probably instigated because the 10th century medieval Yemeni writer al-Hamdani stated that this "wonderful castle...also is the necropolis of the famous kings of Himyar [and] should a tomb be discovered and unearthed, precious stones and money would be found therein." Other bronze statuary discovered here includes a large rearing horse, originally with a rider, and which is now in the Dumbarton Oaks collection, and was apparently found here in 1929. This carries a dedicatory inscription referring to the dedication of two (bronze) horses and riders, by one Hawfatat of the Ghayman tribe to the sanctuary of Madrah. Part of a second bronze horse was found in 1931, along with a second fragmentary bronze head of the same style as this example. If the pieces did form a group of two horses and riders, it is possible that this was a depiction of the young Dioscuri, the divine twins Castor and Pollux of Greek legend, often depicted riding horses. The same identification has been tentatively proposed for the pair of bronze lion riders excavated at Timna, and the astral symbolism of the Diocuri would certainly have appealed to dedicants in Southern Arabia.

Whether the heads belong to the missing riders, is speculative but the fact that two heads exist suggests that they are not portraits of individuals. They have been variously interpreted as representative of youth, men or women, but the corkscrew locks are represented on Sabaean coin portraits from the mid-2nd century bc to mid-3rd century ad, as well as on ancient South Arabian stone statuary, and on murals at Qaryat al-Fau. It is difficult to date the statues exactly, but corkscrew locks were used on Ptolemaic Graeco-Egyptian statuary from the 2nd century bc, and longer curls were in vogue with Roman women in the 1st century bc.

Scientific analysis indicates that this head was made of a leaded bronze, and thus broadly resembles the composition of the Dumbarton Oaks horse and other analyzed late period bronzes from Southern Arabia. However, this is not particularly remarkable, as leaded bronzes were widely used in the Near East and Roman Empire during this period. The Romans tended to use a specific alloy for their life-size statuary bronze which contained over 15% of lead and about 5% of tin, but many examples of statuary bronze containing from 4-12% of lead are also attested. The reason for the addition of lead to the alloy was to make the molten metal more fluid, thereby aiding the casting process. The missing pupils on this head were originally inlaid with another material, which have since become detached: this is a common feature of South Arabian carved stone statuary, but is less commonly seen on metalwork.

The head now has dark corroded hair and a golden metallic face. This is not an original contrast, or the product of different alloys, but is the result of selective conservation, presumably shortly after its discovery, and before it entered The British Museum. The bronze would almost certainly originally have been a deep golden bronze color all over the head, but must have emerged from the ground in a heavily corroded state. The restoration has thereby given it an appearance which it was never intended to have.

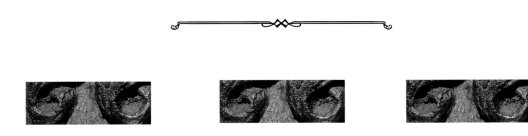

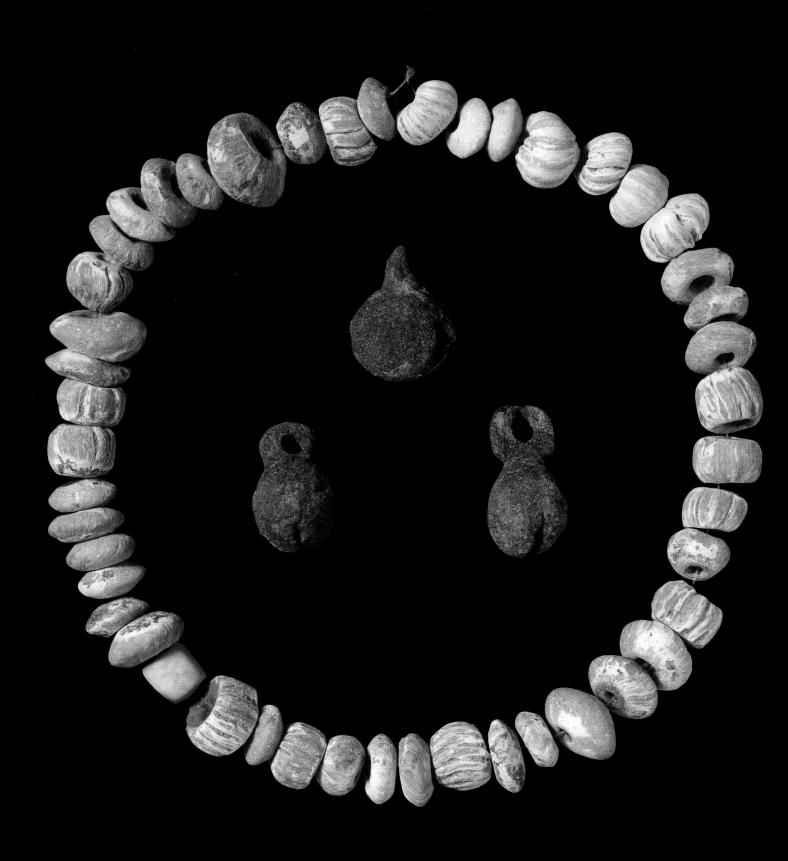

Dress, Jewelry & Seals

"The corpse of a woman wrapped in her shrouds.
On her ankles were two anklets of red gold"
(al-Hamdani).

Dress, jewelry, hairstyles and facial grooming are often indicative of social status or tribal affiliation. However, no traces of ancient clothing survive from Yemen, and textual sources are generally uninformative, although an apology that a female servant had "worn a soiled and threadbare mantle which she had mended in such a way as to hide its flaws from her lords [the gods] Anyat and Samawai," suggests that neatness and tidiness were the socially acceptable norms. Nevertheless, the sculptures offer a useful source of information, and the overall visual appearance of men and women alike, and a small quantity of excavated jewelry helps to illustrate in detail patterns of personal adornment, trade and technology.

Most of the clothing depicted on ancient South Arabian sculpture appears to be loose rather than fitted. This therefore provides an antecedent of traditional Arab dress, which contrasts with fashions in other parts of the Near East. The origin of this, as with all traditions, is probably deeply rooted in practicality, as loose clothing is ideally suited to hot temperatures, and is easily adapted to cooler temperatures through the addition of more layers. One funerary stela from Timna cemetery shows a reclining figure wearing a long gown decorated with an "H" pattern, a type also shown on a second stela in the Musée du Louvre. This was a Roman style known to have been popular in Syria, and as far east as the southern edge of Iraq in the first centuries *ad*, but these depictions add substance to references in the mid-1st century *ad* text, the Periplus of the Erythraean Sea, which refers to the Roman export of fringed mantles, colored cloaks, "Arsinoitic robes," tunics, striped sashes, and unfulled Egyptian cloth to East Africa and Southern Arabia. The reference to the Roman import via the Red Sea port of Mouza, of "Arabian sleeved clothing both unlined and common with check patterns and interwoven with gold...cotton cloth, cloaks, blankets...striped sashes," provide a further hint of the variety of available clothing. Earlier still, individuals carefully depicted on 8th century *bc* pillared sanctuaries in the Jawf, appear to be wearing long skirts decorated with chevrons held at the top with a belt and crossed braces

BEAD, NECKLACE AND BELLS
Glass, bronze
Acquired in Sanaa
Presented by Dr. Sidney E. Croskery

This restrung necklace of green glass melon, short bicone beads, and a single cylindrical disc marble bead, was acquired by the donor in the Yemeni capital at Sanaa in 1942, but possibly dates to the first few centuries *ad*. The composition of the glass has been analyzed in The British Museum, and shown to be similar to melon beads made of faience that have been excavated at Huraydah and Shabwa, and similar green glass bicone beads have also been excavated at Huraydah. In addition, similar bronze bells were found in domestic contexts in level B, dated to the 1st century *bc*-1st century *ad*, at Hajar ibn Humayd, where they were believed to have been strung on a necklace, or less probably, worn as earrings. Others were found in domestic contexts excavated in the Wadi al-Jubah, or in funerary contexts of the same period at Timna, and a necklace consisting of multiple bells is depicted worn around the neck of an ancient South Arabian stone bull gargoyle in the Sanaa National Museum. Finally, the discovery of many other similar bells in graves across southeast Arabia, southern Iran, and even Mesopotamia (modern Iraq), implies that they had a very wide usage.

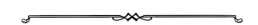

over a plain blouse with long cut sleeves. Finally, another stela, acquired by William Harold Ingrams (b.1897) at Shabwa, shows a winged goddess wearing a short sleeved vertically striped dress with a rounded neckline, which hints at a pre-Islamic production of the famous indigo and yellow ikat-dyed textiles, which Yemen later exported throughout the Islamic world, and which are characterized by creating a distinctive pattern by binding the warp threads to resist the dye prior to weaving.

Silk and cotton are unlikely to have been widely worn prior to the medieval period, although the import of cotton through Mouza is mentioned by the Periplus. Small fragments of woven wool, linen and camel hair cloth have been excavated at Qaryat al-Fau, and linen has been found as wrappings for mummified bodies at Shibam al-Ghiras in Yemen. Depictions on stelae and statuary from the 7th or 6th centuries *bc* -1st century *ad*, suggest that men often wore a plain or fringed kilt made of a single piece of cloth wrapped around the waist, and held in place with a belt. This resembles the traditional Yemeni futah and contrasts with the classical form of toga in which Yasduqil Far Sharahat; a 1st *ad* king of Awsan chose to depict himself.

Double-sided wooden combs have been excavated at Qaryat al-Fau, but evidence for hairstyles and facial grooming is otherwise limited to contemporary representations. Sabaean coins from the 2nd and 1st centuries *bc* suggests that corkscrew locks were a new feature of male hairstyles, which continued at least until the 2nd or mid-3rd centuries *ad*, although the iconography may have fossilized on the later coins. The statuary on the other hand is less closely dated. Nevertheless, female representations suggest the wearing of hair as a single long plait down the back, or elaborately braiding the hair in a series of shoulder length corkscrew locks; a 1st-3rd century *ad* terracotta figurine excavated in the Baran temple at Marib, depicted a seated woman with three plaits running down her back. Men apparently wore small moustaches and/or more commonly, neat and closely trimmed beards, which were indicated on the funerary stelae by rows of drilled dots. A number of statues also suggest that Qatabanian men often wore a stud pierced below the lower lip, unless this is simply an artistic convention for a tuft of hair below the lower lip.

A wide variety of jewelry is depicted on the sculptures and funerary stelae. Men are shown wearing armlets and finger rings, the latter occasionally worn between the first and second joints of the finger, as on Roman sculptures from Palmyra in Syria. Female representations indicate the wearing of single or pairs of bracelets on each wrist, beaded necklaces with triangular pendants, plain torcs, and saltires with prominent central settings clasped by animal-headed terminals. In addition, a stela from the Timna cemetery shows a woman wearing earrings with large pearl drops, a style which was very popular in Mesopotamia and Iran from the 1st century *ad* onward. The source of the pearls was presumably the Gulf of Mannar (India) or the Persian Gulf.

Colored semi-precious stones were worn as settings in saltires or armlets, or strung on necklaces. These have a long local history as carnelian, agate and more locally available varieties of unidentified grey stone beads, are commonly found at Neolithic and Bronze Age sites; beads made of marine shell, including cowrie, dentalium, Strombus, Conus, Pinctada and Engina mendicaria, were popular at sites up to 100 km. inland. Excavated beads from 1st millennium *bc* and later contexts, include agate, amethyst, carnelian, felspar, garnet and granite, and technical analyses of the wear marks inside the drilled perforations of 4th century *bc* or earlier beads from Hajar ar-Rayhani, suggest the use of diamond splinter drills to perforate these hard stones. Softer stones were also used, including calcite, limestone and steatite. Yemen is famous for its chalcedonies, including agate, carnelian and onyx, which occur in volcanic formations in the highlands, from Taizz in the south to Shahara in the north. Others were probably imported as part of Indian Ocean trade with Somalia and south India, the latter being the principal source of the beryl, rock crystal, amethyst, diamonds, almandine garnet, black onyx and probably prase which were supplied at great cost to Rome. It is no surprise to therefore find Diodorus Siculus referring to Arabia as a source of "outcrops of all sorts of gemstones of remarkable color and radiant brilliance." In other cases, it is clear that glass beads were also popular: these were the most common material of beads in the cave-tombs at Huraydah, with colors ranging from red, green and blue, to yellow and orange, yellow and green, black, purple, and white. These colored glass beads were probably regarded as a cheaper means of reproducing the semi-precious hard stones, but whether they were locally made, or were perhaps imported from India or Rome, is uncertain.

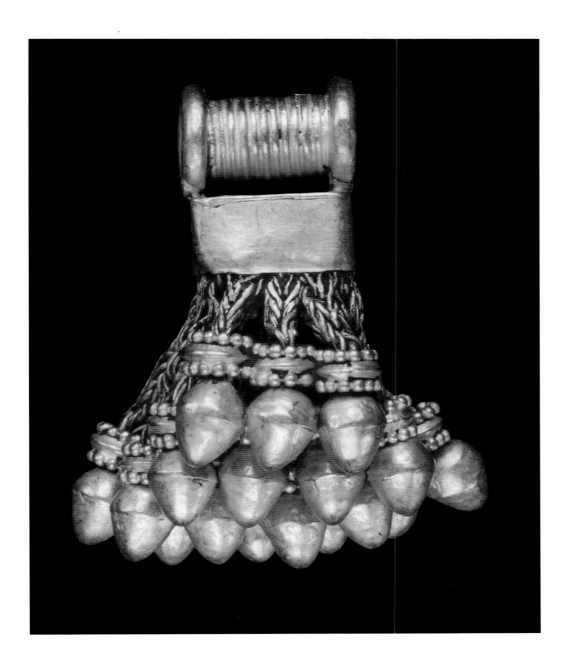

PENDANT
Gold
Possibly from the Wadi Bayhan
Purchased from Nicholas Wright;
a previous owner is said to have been the Emir of Bayhan

This was made with a grooved cotton-reel at the top, with thicker wire at each end attached to a square cloison, holding braided gold strands, ending in a tight cluster of seventeen hollow ovoid acorn-like buds (each made in two halves), attached with shallow hollow drum shaped beads, with short swollen bodies and beaded collars at the top and bottom. Although previously identified as an earring, it appears to be too heavy for this function, and the fitting at the top suggests that it had originally been strung as a pendant.

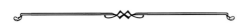

ASSORTED GOLD BEADS
Possibly from the Wadi Bayhan
Purchased from Nicholas Wright; a previous owner
is said to have been the Emir of Bayhan

This group consists of a restrung collection of gold collar beads, many in the basic form of two plain strips alternating with two rings of small granulated spheres. Some are paralleled by other gold beads published from southern and southeast Arabia, suggesting that they were typical of high-class jewelry. Other hollow spherical beads illustrated here were made in two halves, joined at the center, a technique which relied on the use of a metal punch with a hemispherical tip, to stamp tiny gold circles of gold to an identical diameter and depth. The same technique was also used to make 4th century gold jewelry in Greece and Lydia (southwest Turkey), although there is no evidence for a direct link between these and South Arabian craft traditions.

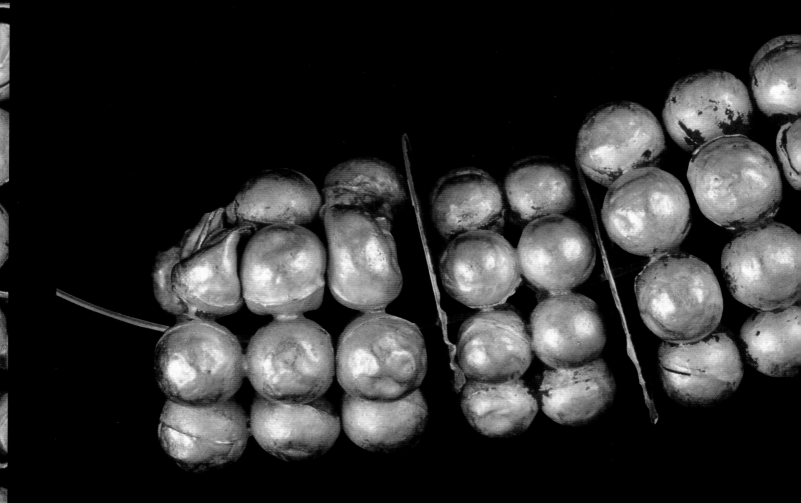

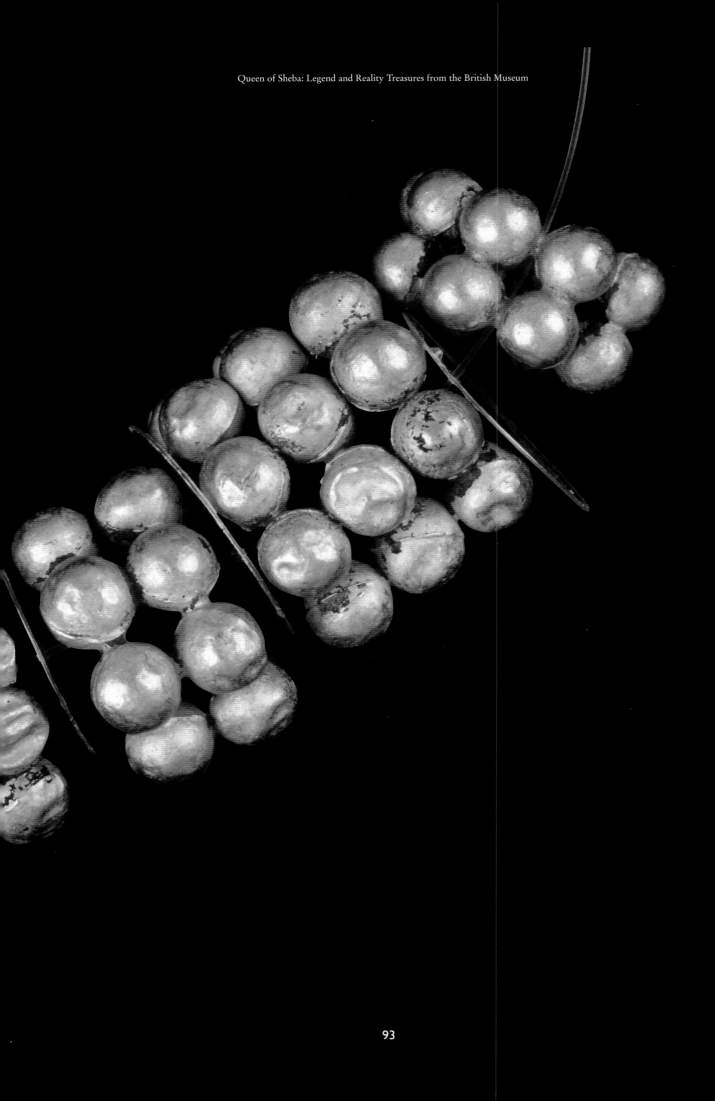

STAMP SEAL SHOWING A CAMEL-RIDER
Carnelian

This translucent carnelian oval seal bezel, originally set in a finger ring, depicts a camel-rider. The rider is seated on or immediately behind the hump of the one-humped variety of camel, known as a dromedary (Camelus dromedarius), and which is indigenous to Arabia. The rider is shown with what may be long plaited hair, but what more probably is intended to be a keffiyeh-like headdress, similar to that depicted on the head of a camel-rider stela in the Musée du Louvre and still widely worn by men across the Middle East. The rider is shown gripping the sides of the camel with his knees, as is typical of riders who do not use stirrups. He holds a stick or goad, appears to be riding bareback, and is guiding the animal by a rope halter attached to its head. The lack of further detail of a harness or a saddle blanket might be explained by the miniature scale of the design. A single South Arabian letter "H" is engraved behind the camel-rider, and has been interpreted as the initial of the rider; alternatively, it may represent the forked lightning emblem of the South Arabian storm god Athtar.

Over 350 South Arabian seals are represented in various museum and private collections, although very few come from archaeological contexts. They are therefore difficult to date exactly, although the form and style of the letters on inscribed seals offer some clues. It is also impossible to tell whether there were chronological or regional developments in the use of seals. However, it appears that seals made of copper alloy, carnelian and agate were the most popular. They were typically perforated lengthways, and some resemble sliced beads, and therefore must have been attached to a cord, perhaps worn around the neck or wrist.

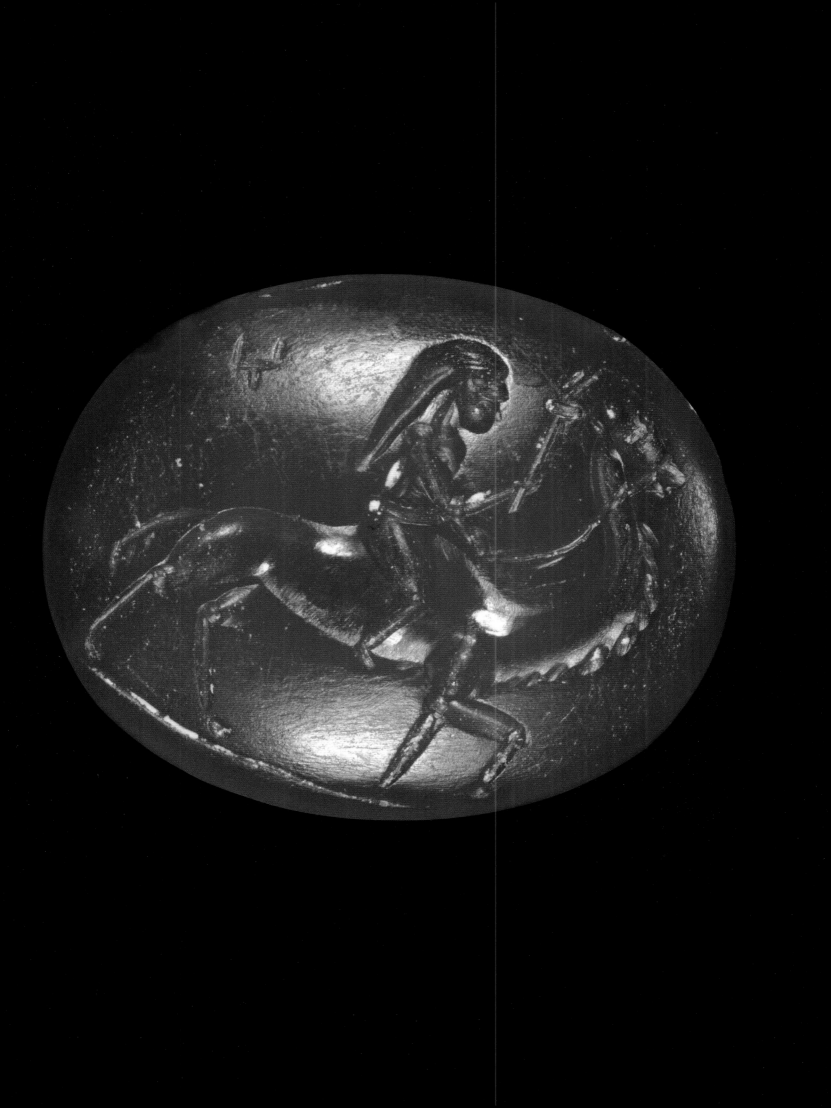

"The pots are so depressingly ugly that a prolonged contemplation
of them would make anyone ill"
(Freya Stark).

Small quantities of fine or brightly colored pottery and glass vessels were imported into Southern Arabia and used there as exotic tablewares. These included Roman glossy red (sigillata) plates, mosaic-glass (millefiori) bowls made in Egypt, and fine Nabataean pottery bowls painted with delicate floral sprays, all imported either via the Red Sea or overland through what is now Saudi Arabia. Some of these imported goods are mentioned in the mid-1st century *ad* source, the Periplus of the Erythraean Sea, which describes the sale of "several sorts of glassware," "imitation murrhine ware made in Diospolis" and "drinking cups" in the Red Sea ports. From the east, came burnished pottery from India which had been decorated before firing with rouletted designs, Parthian pottery bowls and jars from southern Iraq or southwest Iran, which were covered with bright green or blue glaze, tall pottery beakers from southeast Iran which were painted with black designs, and even a thick-walled shallow Sasanian glass bowl decorated all over with deep cut facets. These eastern imports are not mentioned in any historical written accounts, but have been found in archaeological excavations or as chance finds, and may represent part of the cargo of ships returning from northern India or sailing from Persian Gulf ports.

In contrast, the locally manufactured pottery lacked decorative glazes and was invariably handmade and highly utilitarian. Shapes included footed bowls, bowls with pinched "wavy rims," hole-mouth containers, small jars with narrow necks and sharply everted rims, and large storage jars which were sometimes inscribed around the top of the rim. The surface of these pots were sometimes decorated with crudely painted designs or

INSCRIBED "BEEHIVE" JAR
3rd century bc-1st century ad
Calcite-alabaster
Presented by Dr. L.A. Lawrence

This type of calcite-alabaster jar, or so-called "beehive" shaped vessel, has been found at archaeological sites throughout the Arabian Peninsula, including graves on the Persian Gulf island of Bahrain, but the majority have been found in Yemen whence they were made and exported. This vessel has a flat bottom, two pierced handles in the form of highly stylized bull's heads, and two short drilled, dotted Qatabanian inscriptions which give two personal names, "Ammyathi" and "Abkahil." The first of these names also occurs on stone vessels, a gold seal and the base of a statue in the former Muncherjee collection, which was said to have come from a tomb group belonging to one of the kings of Awsan, but the findspot of this jar is unknown. The lid has a handle on the top in the form of stylized animal's head, but the lid does not appear to be original, despite reportedly having been found cemented onto the object before it was acquired. The vessel is also said to have been found containing a hoard of coins, mostly of South Arabian origin, including fifteen silver Himyarite "Bucranium" series coins dating to the 1st century *bc*, six Himyarite Royal series coins dating to *ad* 50-150, a Roman republican silver denarius, and a Roman provincial bronze of Antoninus Pius (*ad* 138-161). The coins have since been dispersed, as the previous owner was a coin collector. This is not the only vessel of this type to have been found in this region and reportedly containing a hoard of coins or jewelry but, if indeed these objects were found in these vessels, it probably simply implies that the latter had been recycled in antiquity (or more recent times), as a convenient container, as vessels of this type were intended as containers for expensive unguents in the form of semi-solid perfumed ointments or animal fat grease.

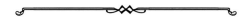

covered with a lightly burnished red ochreous slip. The chronological development of these wares is still largely based on a single archaeological sequence excavated at the site of Hajar ibn Humayd, on the Wadi Bayhan, south of the Qatabanian capital at Timna, albeit increasingly supplemented by smaller single site assemblages. The overall impression is one of a highly conservative tradition of ceramic manufacture, which persisted even in the urban centers where more rapid methods of throwing pots on the wheel might otherwise have been expected. Moreover, it might be added that even at Hajar ibn Humayd, pottery was not as overwhelmingly abundant as it is at contemporary sites in Mesopotamia or the Levant, leading the excavator, Gus van Beek, to comment that it was only 1/400 the quantity of that found during a particular season at Tell Jemmeh.

However, greater effort was paid to making more expensive types of containers from metal or attractive veined calcite-alabaster. The latter was particularly favored for making small "beehive" jars used for storing and transporting sticky unguents, and which were exported to the Persian Gulf and even Mesopotamia (modern Iraq). Cast copper bowls and buckets, carved bone or ivory cosmetic boxes (pyxides), and softstone (steatite) vessels were also used. The latter were carved by hand and traces of the original pick marks can still be seen on the surfaces: some of those excavated at Timna were used for cooking, as they have blackened interiors, protruding ledge handles for lifting in and out of the oven, and a ledge inside the rim for a lid. Doubtless, many more containers were made of organic materials which do not survive as easily, yet fragments of lathe turned wooden bowls, woodwork painted with a marbling effect, and woven palm leaf baskets are attested, and even the shape of the cast metal buckets imitates that of wooden versions held together with metal bands at the top and bottom. The precise function of many of these containers is ambiguous, and some simply represent the ancient equivalent of packaging, whereby the contents rather than the vessel in question were the principal source of interest. Future chemical residue analyses may throw some light on this issue, but the surviving evidence nevertheless demonstrates the types of vessels in use and, indirectly, the trade and distribution mechanisms behind their appearance at ancient sites in Southern Arabia.

RHYTON (WINE-POURER)
Possibly 1st-4th century ad
Pottery
Acquired near Sanaa
Presented by Mrs. Harold Jacob

This is one of two virtually identical vessels which were acquired near the Yemeni capital of Sanaa by the previous owner, presented to The British Museum in 1929, and initially (although wrongly), believed to be Bronze Age in date. The bodies have dark grey fabrics containing burnt out organic temper; a lightly burnished red slip (probably haematite), covers the exterior and extends as far as 7 cm. down the interior. The vessel was lightly incised prior to firing with zig-zag and running spiral designs, and a small bull's head was applied above the tip of the spout, with drilled holes representing the nostrils and other facial features. The appearance of the fabric is totally different to ancient South Arabian, Indian or classical fabrics. Likewise, although bull's heads (bucrania) are a common motif in South Arabian art and architecture, the style of rendering of this particular example is completely different, and lacks the characteristic facial features of ancient South Arabian representations. The actual form of this type of vessel was developed in ancient Iran, and specifically used for serving wine at the table. It is likely that this particular vessel was used for the same purpose, and it may be an Iranian import. If so, this is not the first case where Iranian tablewares have been found in Southern Arabia; fragmentary blue or green-glazed wares from southwest Iran or southern Mesopotamia have been found at Khawr Ruri (the ancient port of Sumhuram), painted and burnished pottery beakers belonging to a southeast Iranian tradition known as "Fine Orange Painted Ware," and datable between the 1st-4th centuries *ad* have been excavated at the South Arabian port of Qana, and an elaborately faceted glass bowl probably dating to the 6th century was apparently found in a grave in the Jawf region of northern Yemen. Viewed together, these vessels provide new evidence for the circulation of Iranian goods in Southern Arabia, and support the fact that Southern Arabia was increasingly being drawn into a complex pattern of trade that began with Red Sea trading links between Egypt and Punt, grew to connect Rome with India, and now saw the beginning of a pattern of Indian Ocean trade documented in the Early Islamic period of connections between Egypt, Southern Arabia, East Africa, Iran, India and the Far East.

LAMP WITH LEAPING IBEX PROTOME
Probably 5th-4th century bc
Bronze
Purchased from Rabi Soleymani; said to have been presented to
a previous owner in Port Sudan

The ibex was a popular decorative motif in South Arabian art and material culture, and there is no reason to doubt that this fine lamp was made locally. The ibex on this particular example has a hole through the right foreleg, which may have been used to suspend an object. This lamp is closely paralleled by a second example from Shabwa in the Kunsthistorisches Museum in Vienna which has a similar protome emerging from a handle in the form of a "Herakles knot," a third example exists in the Musée du Louvre, and a yet more elaborate example was found at Matara in Ethiopia. The date of these lamps is uncertain, but as the protomes are derived from an Achaemenid Persian type and "Herakles knots" were a popular motif in slightly later ancient Greek jewelry, particularly during the second half of the 4th century *bc*, it is likely that they date to the 5th-4th centuries *bc*. A short inscription on the base of the Vienna lamp has been palaeographically dated between the 1st and 3rd centuries *ad*, but this may have been added later.

Scientific analysis has revealed more details on how this lamp was made. The protome and base were cast separately and then joined with rivets, of which three are still extant; two of these are of almost pure copper alloy, whereas the third appears to be of iron and probably represents a later repair. X-ray fluorescence analysis indicates that the object was made of leaded bronze containing traces of arsenic and silver.

Death & Burial

"It was customary [among the Himyarites] to entomb with the dead their riches"
(al-Hamdani).

Deliberate burial of the dead is an essential feature of human behavior. As early as the 10th millennium *bc* early inhabitants of northern Iraq created a cemetery in a cave at Shanidar, and in some cases, even placed beaded necklaces with the dead. Thereafter, during the Neolithic period in the Near East, several key features emerged. Early villagers chose either to bury their dead in organized cemeteries near the edge of the settlement, or place family members below the floors of the occupied houses as if to mark the permanence of association of family with their home. In some cases, the place of burial was distinguished according to whether the individual was an adult or a young child. The provision of items with the deceased also increases in number and variety, beginning with personal jewelry, to including a selection of stone, pottery or (from the Bronze Age), metals containers and other items. This addition of so-called "grave-goods" is normally believed to indicate evidence of ancient beliefs in an afterlife, as most famously exemplified by ancient Egyptian funerary traditions. However, in most other parts of the Near East, there are few literary or religious texts to confirm this hypothesis, and in the case of ancient Mesopotamia, it has been convincingly argued that the buried items are either part of the dress of the deceased or the offerings made by mourners after a funerary feast. Still less is known about the belief system in ancient Southern Arabia, and any interpretation has to be based largely upon archaeological deduction. However, desecration of the place of burial was fundamentally abhorred and feared, hence, the assistance of the god Athtar was specifically invoked for the protection of the dead, and the funerary stela of Yasduqil Far Sharahat, a 1st century *ad* king of Awsan, forbade its removal by any later kings, stating: "let it remain in this place for all time to come."

Excavations within Southern Arabia confirm considerable variety in ancient burial customs, ranging from the construction of stone cairn or "turret tombs," cave tombs, subterranean hypogeal or multistory tower-tombs shared by many individuals assumed to belong to single families, to cist graves containing a single body placed in a flexed or extended position. The earliest of these traditions are the so-called cairn or "turret tombs," which extend from parts of the western highlands through the desert margins in the northern part of Yemen and along natural routes into other parts of Arabia. The smaller of these were circular stone constructions, with a single door less chamber roofed with capstones, and occasionally with stone stelae set upright in the outer

MALE HEAD
Possibly 3rd-2nd century bc
Calcite-alabaster
Probably from Hayd ibn Aqil
Presented by Sir Charles Johnston (1912-1986)

The neatly trimmed beard framing the long oval face is indicated with a row of short incised lines; the eyes are represented with shell inlays, with the pupils originally represented by separate colored stone inlays, which have since become detached. The eyebrows were also originally inlaid, and the shallow circular depression below the lower lip appears to mark the position of yet another missing inlay, implying that studs were a feature of male fashion in ancient South Arabia. The top, back and sides of the head were deliberately left unfinished, as the head was originally set into a niche within a tomb and thus these parts would not have been visible.

This sculptured head was presented by the Emir of Bayhan to Sir Charles Johnston, a British career diplomat, during the course of his posting as Governor and Commander-in-Chief of the British colony in Aden between 1960 and 1963. It was reportedly from the "ruins of Timna," but was probably found in the nearby cemetery at Hayd ibn Aqil, rather than the main city site.

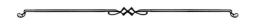

wall, which were carved to represent a human figure wearing a short sword. Larger so-called "turret tombs" measured up to 3.5 m. high, and included a doorway to facilitate repeated use. Investigations at Jabal Jidran and Ruwaiq indicate that these tombs were already used in the Bronze Age during the 3rd millennium *bc*, although some may have been constructed earlier, and others continued to be reused for centuries. These tombs were typically accompanied by curious long tail-like alignments of smaller tombs, cairns, platforms and other structural features. Later graves from the Jawf region appear to have contained or been marked with stelae simply representing the face and short name, whereas others appear to have contained small limestone statuettes depicting a man or woman seated on a small chair, which belong to a type also carved from calcite-alabaster in the Timna cemetery.

The cave tombs are most typical of the Hadramawt region in eastern Yemen and the highlands. Excavations of one such tomb at Huraydah in 1938 by Gertrude Caton-Thompson (1888-1985), revealed the remains of up to forty-two men, women and children accompanied by as many as eighty-seven pots, as well as beads, shell containers or scoops and obsidian microliths within a roughly circular tomb measuring some 8 m. across. The tomb therefore appeared to have been used over a long period of time between the 7th and 5th centuries *bc*, perhaps by members of a single clan, with the decaying remains of each interment being gathered together and put into a separate pile to make room for the next burial, the most recent apparently being placed on a rock-cut bench immediately inside the tomb entrance. Similar periodic reuse was found in a rock-cut tomb at Shabwa where unusually the facade was highlighted with red painted sculptures set within rectangular niches. At other sites in the same region dating between the last centuries *bc* and first centuries *ad*, some burials were accompanied by sacrificed camels. These have been interpreted in the light of pre-Islamic Arab poems as the favorite mounts required by the deceased on the day of resurrection, and belong to a wider tradition found during this period in eastern Arabia as well as in Sudan. It is unlikely that these simply represent the graves of cameleers involved in the caravan trade, but more probably, witness the greater economic and status value of the camel during this period in Arabia as a provider of milk, wool and meat as well as a means of transport.

There is also extensive evidence for deliberate mummification of the dead, principally in the highlands of Yemen, which apparently involved at least partial evisceration of the corpse, packing the body cavity with woad, aromatic substances, and the flowers and seeds of a local plant desiccant called Raa, and carefully wrapping the clothed body in finely woven linen held together with leather bands or enclosed within a stitched leather sack. These bodies were usually placed on high rock ledges or inside artificial cave tombs, most notably at the site of Shibam al-Ghiras where five body bundles were found to contain carefully stitched leather shoes and were accompanied by miniature carved wooden statuettes, amulets, an iron spearhead, a leather shoulder bag and a possible slingshot. Carbon-14 dating suggests that this group of burials may date to the mid-1st millennium *bc*. There is also evidence for the burial of mummies in constructed "turret tombs" near Marib. However, this practice appears to be unique in the Near East outside Egypt, and strongly suggests the diffusion of this funerary concept from that country, and where the mummified corpse of a 3rd century *bc* Minaean merchant called Zaydil bin Zayd was found inside in a wooden sarcophagus at Memphis, opposite Thebes.

However, it is the extramural urban cemeteries of Marib and Timna, although still only partially explored or published, which offer perhaps the most evocative insights into the world of the dead, as well as being the source of most of the carved stone statuettes and stelae in public and private collections. The tombs at Timna each stood up to a height of 4 m. and were constructed in rows terraced into the side of a small mountain with a temple at the foot. Each tomb contained up to eight rooms opening onto a central corridor, with each room containing at least three superimposed rectangular loculi measuring up to 2 m. in length. These loculi were designed for individual interments and were sealed at the mouth with a stone slab. The overall appearance of these tombs was therefore akin to a modern morgue. One inscription found in this cemetery is particularly interesting as it commemorates the construction of a shared tomb for Minaeans resident in Timna and states how it was "immune" to reuse by others: "Awsal, the son of Lahayathat, of the clan RWYN, the chief of Main in Timna, and Main [who are] residents of Timna, built and raised high and renewed their burial place, the 'Immune,' from [the] foundation to [the] top as [their] property in agreement with [various named local clans]."

A different style of funerary architecture was developed at Marib, where the tombs were constructed of tufa or limestone blocks with carefully dressed ashlar facades, and the inner walls covered with red painted clay or lime plaster. These tombs are estimated to have originally stood to a height of up to 10 m., contained three or four floors with wooden or stone shelves to support the corpses, and held up to two hundred bodies each. The remains of men and women, with a smaller proportion of children, were found. Growth within the cemetery was vertical, and new floors were constructed above old ones when tombs became full. This necessitated the construction of steep central staircases or sets of wooden steps, as well as the blocking of the original entrances. The more important tombs here were constructed with a columned peristyle or portico raised on a podium, and thus resembled the facades of small temples. Some were inscribed with the personal name, clan or tribe, and occasionally rank of the owners, some of whom were stated to be a tribal chief or priest; some inscriptions indicate that chambers could be purchased or rented, rather like the shared tombs at Palmyra in Syria. Other external facades were crudely carved with the faces of deceased family members. This cemetery lasted approximately from at least the 8th century *bc* to the 4th century *ad*, although the main period of use was between the 6th and 3rd centuries *bc*. It extended over an area of some 1.7 hectares and is estimated to have contained a total of as many as 20,000-30,000 burials. The fact that there was evidence for careful resurfacing of the alleys separating the rows of tombs suggests that there was some degree of municipal or religious involvement in its maintenance; its immediate proximity to the Awwam temple, which it enveloped on the southern side, has been interpreted as evidence for a close relationship between religious and funerary customs. Alternatively it may simply reflect deep-seated traditional beliefs, whereby burial close to "sacred ground" offered apotropaic protection for the "houses of the dead."

However, at both sites it is impossible to reliably reconstruct the full range of funerary contents, or the ceremonies involved, as the shelves collapsed and the tombs were repeatedly looted over subsequent centuries. Among the excavated finds at Marib are miniature stone, metal and pottery versions of incense burners, altars, libation tables and containers, which suggest that scaled down versions of ritually important objects were produced specifically for funerary use. The discovery of bracelets, necklaces, rings and small glazed faience pendants suggests that the corpses were accompanied by personal jewelry and amulets. Additional finds included red painted terracotta figurines of camels, female figures with outstretched arms that perhaps represent dedicants, and glazed faience Ushabti tomb-model figures of Egyptian type, but probably imported in the Levant. Occasional traces of burning were found within the tombs or in the alleys at both Marib and Timna, but the causes of these are uncertain. However, they do explain the occasional signs of blackening found on some of the funerary sculptures from these sites.

The most distinctive finds from the cemeteries are the stelae. These range considerably in type, but typically depict the stylized face and rarely the bust of a man or woman (but never a child), carved from a beautiful veined calcite-alabaster, and which was often set with colored inlays of shell, stone and glass, or occasionally with metal jewelry attached. The top of the head or the dotted representation of a beard was occasionally highlighted with lampblack, but otherwise the use of pigment was surprisingly rare. The stylization of the faces has been interpreted as evidence that they were intended to be symbolic and ageless portraits, yet paradoxically there is a considerable variety of style and individualism within the genre which is more than simply variable skill or disposable wealth. The top, sides and back of these heads were left flat and were only roughly trimmed as they were originally either placed within niches constructed within the tomb, or cemented into niches cut into the tops of individual rectangular stela blocks which were apparently set up against the exterior facades in the Marib cemetery. Some of these rectangular stela blocks were later recycled as convenient building material within the cemetery, and many others are missing the heads, which had either been removed in antiquity or in more recent times. However, following the discovery of as many as fourteen intact examples during recent German excavations at the site, it has been proposed that the inlaid heads were originally protected behind small hinged wooden or metal doors. In this case it seems likely that the faces were exposed during particular ceremonies connected with commemoration of the deceased.

Other distinctive types of stelae which are particularly represented from the Timna cemetery consist of larger standing or seated figures, again carved from calcite-alabaster, and which depict the drapery or facial features in slightly more detail, small heads set into inscribed bases, or simply masks made of fired clay or plaster. Another category, previously described as "goddess plaques," but now believed to represent the deceased or the dedicant, depict draped female figures with one hand raised and the other typically holding a sheaf of grain, or a man in profile clutching a sword. Finally, other Qatabanian stelae were carved in a form resembling a stylized obelisk, or depict a bull's head in high relief.

The collapse of the Sabaean and Qatabanian political capitals at Marib and Timna were followed by the abandonment of these urban cemeteries in the 4th and 1st centuries *ad* respectively. In other parts of Southern Arabia, burial appears to have increasingly been within simpler individual cist graves cut into the soil, and often with a smaller range of objects placed with the deceased. A particularly rich exception, were a small group of graves excavated in the Wadi Dura, and which contained ivory, silver and gold tablewares and imported Roman glass vessels. The adoption of Roman forms of banqueting has also been interpreted as the reason for the appearance in the Timna cemetery at Hayd ibn Aqil of a small number of stelae depicting figures reclining on couches, accompanied by female musicians and surrounded by classical acanthus and vine scroll motifs. In contrast, the increasing popularity of cist graves have sometimes been interpreted as evidence for the immigration of Arab-speaking or nomad tribes into this region in the first few centuries *ad*, but may alternatively be viewed as part of a wider burial phenomenon within the Near East or Roman Mediterranean, and which partly reflects the effect of Jewish and Christian religious beliefs. However, the increasing penetration of Arabic speakers is attested by the appearance of northern Arab names on so-called "eye stelae" found from the Jawf in the north, to Timna and other sites in the Wadi Bayhan. These stelae consisted of small rectangular limestone or wooden blocks simply depicting a nose and eyes, the latter often stylized as lozenges or semi-circles, inscribed with the name of the deceased, occasionally highlighted with colored pigment and trimmed at the back for insertion into the tomb wall.

Sadly, stories of treasures buried in the ancient tombs of Yemen excited early Islamic authors and later folk legends with descriptions of the discovery of "jewels the like of which none had seen, and...gold and silver." Such reports stimulated local governors "to send out expeditions to the tombs to secure their buried treasures, because it was customary [among the Himyarites] to entomb with the dead their riches." The purpose of these expeditions was therefore to plunder the tombs so that the precious metals and gemstones could be melted or recarved. Al-Hamdani continues by describing a specific case of this whereby "we then took away the gold...and delivered it to the governor, who rewarded me with a hundred dinars. With it I decorated my [gold] sword." Archaeological excavations of tombs and cemeteries throughout Yemen indicate similar widespread looting which continued until recent times.

FUNERARY STELA
Probably 1st century bc
Calcite-alabaster
Probably from the Timna cemetery at Hayd ibn Aqil
Purchased from Spink & Son; previously owned by Johannes, Bishop of Ryswick

This stela is a beautiful example of a particular style of South Arabian dedicatory stela, which depicts the bust of a female in low relief against a square plaque, with an inscription on the low stepped base naming a person, who has been interpreted as either that of the person represented (although other scholars have identified this as representing a goddess), or the dedicant who offered the stela. The figure is shown in a characteristic pose, with the right hand raised and the left hand holding a stylized sheaf of wheat, a symbol of fertility. In similar examples from other collections, the right hand covers the left hand, which holds the wheat, whereas others show the figure holding a bird in the left hand. The grooved eyebrows and drilled irises were originally inlaid, while the holes in the ears indicate that the figure originally wore earrings, presumably of metal. The figure is depicted as wearing a pair of plain bracelets on each wrist, and is wearing a plain short sleeved tunic with raised hems and a rounded neckline, although she is not wearing the elaborate necklace which is depicted on some other stelae of this type. The statue finishes at the hairline, and the top of the head and the hair are not depicted: this has been suggested as evidence that these details were rendered in plaster or that she wore an artificial wig, but it is more likely that it simply reflects the outline of the wall niche into which this stela is believed to have originally stood. The inscription on the base reads: "Abram daughter of Mahdaram." Previously believed to date to the 2nd century *ad* on the basis of similar frontal depictions in the art of Palmyra and Dura in Roman Syria, it has been reattributed a 1st century *bc* date on the basis of the style of the lettering of the inscription. Traces of accidental burning at the top suggest that the place where it was found had been previously subjected to a fire.

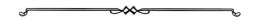

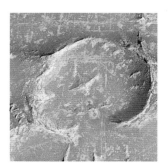

INSCRIBED FUNERARY STELA WITH CAMEL-RIDERS
1st-3rd centuries ad
Calcite-alabaster
Purchased from Charles Albert Brenchley through George Hallett

This stela depicts a camel and two riders, one wearing a kilt or short skirt and brandishing a sword, with a two line Sabaean inscription above which reads "figure and monument of Haan, son of dhu-Zud." A similar funerary stela in the Musée du Louvre also shows a camel-rider who is named in the inscription as "Mushayqarum Hamayat son of Yashuf," and who is shown seated on a saddle placed across the hump, with a waterskin slung next to the left rear flank, and is guiding the camel with a halter and stick.

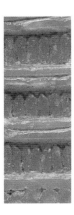

FUNERARY STELA
1st century ad
Calcite-alabaster
Said to be from Hajar ibn Humayd
Presented by Jonathan Hassell

This stela was formerly known as the "Aylward stela," after a previous owner, one Captain John Aylward of the Royal Engineers, who acquired it during military service in Aden during the 1950s. It depicts an amply proportioned lady wearing a long dress decorated down the front with two narrow vertical panels, who is depicted playing a lyre while sitting on a straight-backed chair with her feet resting on a matching foot stool. This figure is flanked on either side by a smaller figure either representing a girl or woman, one of whom may be singing while the other is holding a drum. This probably belongs to a type constructed by tightly stretching a piece of skin over a wooden frame, a method which is still found in parts of the Near East. The figures are depicted below a curving arch, ending in dragon's heads with foliage above, and supported by fluted columns with decorative capitals and flared fluted bases. The identity of the seated figure is uncertain: she has been identified as a goddess, but the funerary context of this series instead suggests that she is the subject of the dedication.

This stela resembles another example in The British Museum, which was found at or near the Awwam Temple (or the adjoining cemetery) at Marib, prior to 1870, and which has a very similar upper register, plus a Sabaean inscription which reads: "Image of Ghalilat, daughter of Mufiddat and may Athtar destroy he who breaks it." Another stela of this type in the Musée du Louvre shows a woman with a similar "H" pattern dress seated on a folding stool in front of a folding table loaded, with vessels presumably filled with food and drink, and being waited on by another figure to the sound of music being played on a lute. The series therefore appear to represent banqueting scenes. Although it has been suggested that these were originally fixed onto the walls of temples, the inscription on the Musée du Louvre stela proves a funerary context as it reads: "Image and funerary monument of Iglum son of Saadillat the Qaryote but Athtar Shariqan smites those who damage it."

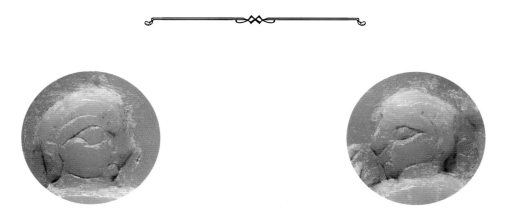

Selected Further Reading

Within the past decade, there have been several general syntheses and well-illustrated exhibition catalogues, listed below. Much of the academic literature about ancient South Arabia is either in academic journals, such as *Arabian Archaeology & Epigraphy* or the *Proceedings of the Seminar for Arabian Studies*, archaeological site reports, and the series Archäologische Berichte aus dem Yemen [ABADY], or publications devoted to South Arabian inscriptions, notably the *Corpus Inscriptionum Semiticarum* [CIS], *Pars Quarta: Inscriptions himyariticas et* Sabaeas published between 1889 and 1932, or the *Répertoire d'Epigraphie Sémitique* [RES] published in seven volumes with an index from 1900 onward. Two archaeological maps of Southern Arabia have been published, the first by Groom & Beeston (1976), and the second by Robin & Brunner (1997), details of which are listed below. Good popular websites with links include http://www.arabianseminar.org.uk.

Breton, J-F. (1999). *Arabia Felix from the Time of the Queen of Sheba: Eighth Century BC to First Century* AD. Notre Dame, Indiana: University of Notre Dame Press. (Translated from the French by Albert LaFarge).

Budge, E.A.W. (1922). *The Queen of Sheba & her only son Menyelek*. London: The Medici Society.

Calvet, Y. & Robin, C., with the assistance of Briquel-Chatonnet, F. & Pic, M. (1997). *Arabie heureuse. Arabie déserte. Les antiquités arabiques du musée du Musée du Louvre*. Paris: Editions de la Réunion des musées nationaux.

Clapp, N. (2001). *Sheba: Through the Desert in Search of the Legendary Queen*. Boston/New York: Houghton Mifflin.

Daum, W. (1988). *Die Königin von Saba*. Stuttgart/Zürich: Belser Verlag.

Daum, W., ed. (1988). *Yemen. 3000 Years of Art and Civilization in Arabia Felix*. Frankfurt am Main: Pinguin.

Doe, B. (1971). *Southern Arabia*. New York: McGraw-Hill.

Groom, N. (1981). *Frankincense and Myrrh. A Study of the Arabian Incense Trade*. London: Longman.

Groom, N. St J. & Beeston, A.F.L. (1976). *A Sketch-map of Southwest Arabia, 1: 1,000,000*. London: The Royal Geographical Society.

Maigret, A. de. (2002). *Arabia Felix. An Exploration of the Archaeological history of Yemen*. London: Stacey International.

Philby, St J. (1981). *The Queen of Sheba*. London: Quartet Books.

Pritchard, J. B., ed. (1974). *Solomon & Sheba*. London: Phaidon Press Ltd.

Robin, C. & Brunner, U. (1997). *Map of Ancient Yemen / Carte du Yémen Antique*. Munich: Staatliches Museum für Völkerkunde.

Robin, C. & Vogt, B., eds. (1997). *Yémen, au pays de la reine de Saba*. Paris: Flammarion.

Simpson, St J., ed. (2002). *Queen of Sheba: Treasures from ancient Yemen*. London: British Museum Press.

Warner, M. (1994). *From the Beast to the Blonde: On fairy tales and their tellers*. London: Chatto & Windus.

Philby, St J. (1981). *The Queen of Sheba*. London: Quartet Books.